ON A ROLL

14 QUILTS THAT START WITH 2½" STRIPS

compiled by
LISSA ALEXANDER

Martingale®
Create with Confidence

Moda All-Stars
On a Roll: 14 Quilts That Start with 2½" Strips
© 2019 by Martingale & Company

Martingale®
19021 120th Ave. NE, Ste. 102
Bothell, WA 98011-9511 USA
ShopMartingale.com

Printed in China
24 23 22 21 20 19   8 7 6 5 4 3 2

Library of Congress Cataloging-in-Publication Data is available upon request.

ISBN: 978-1-60468-988-4

MISSION STATEMENT

We empower makers who use fabric and yarn to make life more enjoyable.

CREDITS

**PUBLISHER AND
CHIEF VISIONARY OFFICER**
Jennifer Erbe Keltner

CONTENT DIRECTOR
Karen Costello Soltys

DESIGN MANAGER
Adrienne Smitke

MANAGING EDITOR
Tina Cook

PRODUCTION MANAGER
Regina Girard

TECHNICAL EDITOR
Nancy Mahoney

BOOK DESIGNER
Angie Hoogensen

COPY EDITOR
Durby Peterson

PHOTOGRAPHER
Brent Kane

ILLUSTRATOR
Lisa Lauch

SPECIAL THANKS
Photography for this book was taken at:

*The home of Kirsten Yanasak of Everett, Washington
(Instagram: @brightyellowdoor)*

*The home of Tracie Fish of Bothell, Washington
(Instagram: @fishtailcottage)*

*The Garden Barn of Indianola, Iowa
(Instagram: @gardenbarn)*

contents

introduction

Let the good times roll! With a Jelly Roll from Moda Fabrics, the good times are sure to do just that. After all, what could be more fun than 40 assorted 2½"-wide precut strips ready and waiting for you in your sewing room? Well, perhaps the 14 quilt patterns that follow! You'll find page after page of inspiration for ways to stitch stunning quilts that start with Jelly Rolls.

The Moda All-Stars—our fabulous team of designers that inspire the fabrics you love—keep rollin' out the projects you love to sew. They can't stop and we hope you won't stop either!

As always, royalties from this book are donated to a charitable organization. School on Wheels' mission is to enhance educational opportunities for homeless children from kindergarten through twelfth grade. Today, hundreds of volunteers work one-on-one with children whose homelessness prevents them from getting the academic stability and help they desperately need.

We know quilters have big hearts, so thank you for your purchase of this book. The donation we make on your behalf will make a difference to homeless children, letting them know they are cared about and important. (Learn more at SchoolOnWheels.org.)

Now grab your Jelly Rolls and let's get quilting! Are you ready to roll?

~ Lissa Alexander

not too sweet

BY SANDY KLOP

*Setting blocks in diagonal rows takes your strips down a different path.
Not Too Sweet is perfect on a table and also makes a great throw!*

FINISHED QUILT: 57" × 68⅜"
FINISHED BLOCKS: 8" × 8"

materials

*Yardage is based on 42"-wide fabric. Jelly Rolls contain
40 strips, 2½" × width of fabric.*

1 Jelly Roll of assorted dark prints for blocks and
setting triangles

2¾ yards *total* of assorted light prints for blocks
and setting triangles

½ yard of pink stripe for binding

3½ yards of fabric for backing

63" × 75" piece of batting

cutting

From *each* of 30 dark print strips, cut:
2 rectangles, 2½" × 8½" (60 total)
2 rectangles, 2½" × 4½" (60 total)
4 squares, 2½" × 2½" (120 total)

From *each* remaining dark print strip, cut:
2 squares, 2½" × 2½" (20 total; 2 will be extra)

From the light prints, cut a *total* of:
4 strips, 4½" × 42"; crosscut into 30 squares, 4½" × 4½"
23 strips, 2½" × 42"; crosscut into:
    58 rectangles, 2½" × 8½"
    44 rectangles, 2½" × 4½"
    18 rectangles, 2½" × 6½"
2 squares, 4⅞" × 4⅞"; cut in half diagonally to yield
    4 triangles

From the pink stripe, cut:
7 strips, 2¼" × 42"

making the blocks

Press all seam allowances in the direction indicated by
the arrows.

1 Sew dark 2½" × 4½" rectangles to the top and
bottom of a light 4½" square. Sew dark 2½" × 8½"
rectangles to opposite sides of the square to make
block A. Make 30 blocks that measure 8½" square,
including seam allowances.

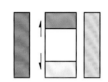

Block A.
Make 30 blocks, 8½" × 8½".

2 Join four dark 2½" squares to make a four-patch
unit. Make 20 units that measure 4½" square,
including seam allowances.

Make 20 units,
4½" × 4½".

3 Sew light 2½" × 4½" rectangles to the top and
bottom of a four-patch unit. Sew light 2½" × 8½"
rectangles to opposite sides of the unit to make block B.
Make 20 blocks that measure 8½" square, including
seam allowances.

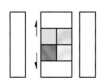

Block B.
Make 20 blocks, 8½" × 8½".

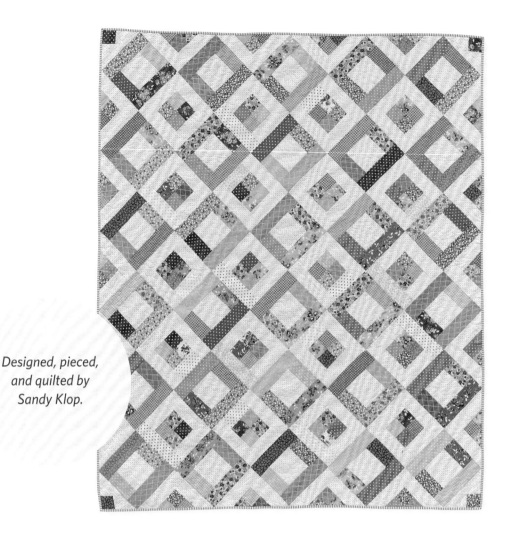

Designed, pieced, and quilted by Sandy Klop.

making the setting triangles

1 Join three dark 2½" squares as shown. Make 18 units.

Make 18.

2 Sew a light 2½" × 6½" rectangle to the bottom of a unit from step 1. Sew a light 2½" × 8½" rectangle to the right side of the unit to make a side triangle. Make 18.

Make 18.

3 Sew a dark 2½" square to one end of a light 2½" × 4½" rectangle. Sew a light triangle to the left side of the unit to make a corner triangle. Make four.

Make 4.

assembling the quilt top

1 Lay out the A and B blocks in diagonal rows, alternating the blocks as shown in the quilt assembly diagram on page 9. Add the side and corner triangles around the perimeter. Sew the blocks and side triangles into rows. Join the rows and add the corner triangles last.

2 Trim and square up the quilt top, making sure to leave ¼" beyond the points of all the blocks for seam allowances. Stitch around the perimeter of the quilt top, ⅛" from the outer edges, to lock the seams in place. The quilt top should measure 57" × 68⅜".

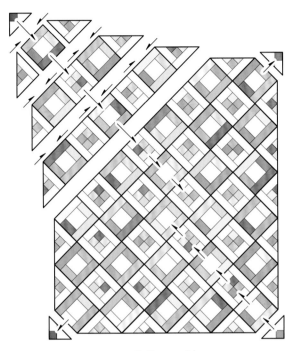

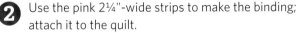
Quilt assembly

finishing the quilt

For more details about any finishing steps, visit ShopMartingale.com/HowtoQuilt.

1 Layer the quilt top, batting, and backing. Hand or machine quilt. Not Too Sweet is quilted with an allover meandering design.

2 Use the pink 2¼"-wide strips to make the binding; attach it to the quilt.

chain reaction

BY LYNNE HAGMEIER

Like riding a bike, once you learn how to piece this way, you'll never forget! Lynne's clever strip-piecing trick keeps the cogs on your Jelly Roll "chain" lined up and uniform, just like a bicycle chain.

FINISHED QUILT: 62½" × 76½"
FINISHED BLOCK: 6" × 8"

materials

Yardage is based on 42"-wide fabric. Jelly Rolls contain 40 strips, 2½" × width of fabric. Fat eighths measure 9" × 21".

1 Jelly Roll of assorted tan and dark prints for blocks

1 or 2 fat eighths of tan prints for blocks*

2 yards of tan print for blocks and sashing

2⅛ yards of navy print for sashing units, border, and binding

4⅝ yards of fabric for backing

69" × 83" piece of batting

*You will need 1 or 2 tan fat eighths only if your Jelly Roll has fewer than 12 tan strips.

cutting

From the assorted dark strips, cut a *total* of:
96 rectangles, 2½" × 8½" (A)

From the assorted tan strips and fat eighths, cut a *total* of:
48 rectangles, 2½" × 8½" (B)

From the tan print for blocks and sashing, cut:
26 strips, 2½" × 42"; crosscut *16 strips* into:
    16 strips, 2½" × 8½" (D)
    192 squares, 2½" × 2½" (C)

From the navy print, cut:
2 strips, 2½" × 42"; crosscut into 32 squares, 2½" × 2½" (E)

From the remaining navy print, cut on the *lengthwise* grain:
2 strips, 6½" × 64½"
2 strips, 6½" × 62½"
5 strips, 2¼" × 60"

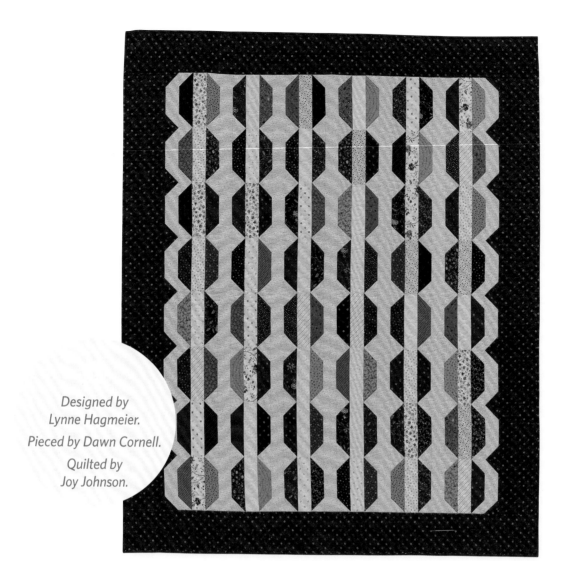

*Designed by
Lynne Hagmeier.
Pieced by Dawn Cornell.
Quilted by
Joy Johnson.*

making the blocks

Press all seam allowances in the direction indicated by the arrows.

1 Sew A rectangles to opposite sides of a B rectangle to make a strip unit. Make 48 units that measure 6½" × 8½", including seam allowances. Note that you will press the seam allowances toward the B rectangle on 24 units and toward the A rectangles on 24 units.

Make 24 of each unit,
6½" × 8½".

2 Draw a diagonal line from corner to corner on the wrong side of each C square. Pin a marked square on one corner of a strip unit, right sides together. Stitch on the drawn line. Trim the outside corner ¼" from the stitched line. In the same way, sew C squares to the remaining three corners of the unit to make a Chain block. Make 48 blocks that measure 6½" × 8½", including seam allowances.

Make 48 blocks,
6½" × 8½".

making the side sashing strips

1 Draw a diagonal line from corner to corner on the wrong side of each E square. Pin marked squares on both ends of a D strip, right sides together, making sure to orient the marked line as shown. Stitch on the drawn line. Trim the outside corner ¼" from the stitched line. Make 16 sashing units that measure 2½" × 8½", including seam allowances.

Make 16 units,
2½" × 8½".

2 Join eight sashing units end to end to make a side sashing strip that measures 2½" × 64½", including seam allowances. Make two strips.

Make 2 strips,
2½" × 64½".

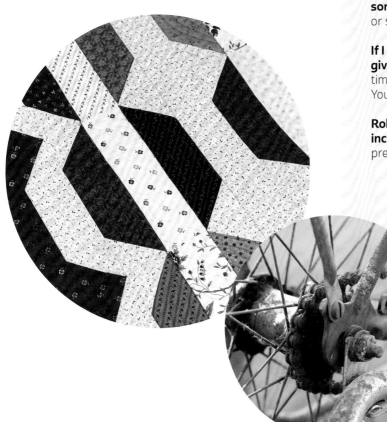

ROLLIN' WITH
Lynne Hagmeier

She's often found rolling along the Midwest highways and byways where antique hidden gems and fabulous finds await her. But there's no place like home for Kansas Troubles Quilters' Lynne Hagmeier (KTQuilts.com) to do her best designing!

When I'm sewing with a Jelly Roll, this is how I roll: It depends on the project, but usually I have to lay out all the strips to see the ratio of light to dark and the mix of print sizes before I go much further.

My favorite roll is a cinnamon roll with pecans.

In my dreams, the car I roll up the driveway in is tough to say. There are sunny days when I daydream about my old Mazda Miata, but my hips appreciate my new Jeep Cherokee.

When I'm on a roll in my sewing room, I turn on Netflix and tell my husband, Robert, it's his turn to make dinner.

Don't roll your eyes, but I seldom change the color of thread in my bobbin.

If I'm rolling up my sleeves and getting ready for some serious sewing time, I make sure to wind five or six bobbins at one time and go!

If I could roll back the clock, here's the advice I'd give my younger self: Don't wait for the perfect time to follow your dreams. Jump off that cliff now. You'll find your wings.

Roll call for my "Sewing Must-Haves" would include these three things: Aurifil thread, a wool pressing mat, and a gallon of chai tea.

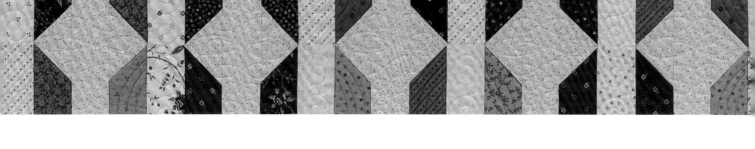

assembling the quilt top

1 Lay out the blocks in six columns of eight blocks each, alternating the blocks with the seam allowances pressed toward A and the blocks with the seam allowances pressed toward B. Sew the blocks together into columns that measure 6½" × 64½", including seam allowances.

2 Join two tan 2½" × 42" strips end to end to make a long strip. Make five pieced sashing strips and trim them to measure 64½" long.

3 Join the columns and sashing strips from step 2, alternating them as shown in the quilt assembly diagram below.

4 Sew the side sashing strips to opposite sides of the quilt center, rotating the strips so that the navy triangles are along the outer edges. The quilt-top center should measure 50½" × 64½", including seam allowances.

5 Sew navy 64½"-long strips to opposite sides of the quilt-top center. Sew navy 62½"-long strips to the top and bottom of the quilt top. The quilt top should measure 62½" × 76½".

Adding borders

Quilt assembly

finishing the quilt

For more details about any finishing steps, visit ShopMartingale.com/HowtoQuilt.

1 Layer the quilt top, batting, and backing. Hand or machine quilt. Chain Reaction is quilted in the ditch between blocks, sashing strips, and borders. A triple curve is quilted in the dark chain strips, a curlicue in the tan strips, and a figure eight in the tan sashing strips. Zigzag lines are quilted in the navy border.

2 Use the navy 2¼"-wide strips to make the binding; attach it to the quilt.

what's the commotion

BY LISA BONGEAN

It's all about creating a look with lots of motion, and this beauty is as tactile as it is luscious to look at. The soft-as-butter quilt is made from flannel plaids and prints and is simple to sew—it's comprised of three easy blocks that twist and turn to create a stunning quilt. An overall fan quilting design creates the perfect rounded finish.

FINISHED QUILT: 48½" × 48½"
FINISHED BLOCKS: 4" × 4"

materials

Yardage is based on 42"-wide flannel fabric. Jelly Rolls contain 40 strips, 2½" × width of fabric.

1 Jelly Roll of assorted dark flannel prints and plaids for blocks

1 yard *each* of 2 different light flannel prints (A and B) for blocks

½ yard of maroon plaid flannel for binding

3⅛ yards of fabric for backing

55" × 55" piece of batting

Template plastic

cutting

From light flannel print A, cut:
13 strips, 2½" × 42"

From light flannel print B, cut:
12 strips, 2½" × 42"

From the maroon plaid flannel, cut:
6 strips, 2¼" × 42"

use two background prints

Choosing a single color for your background doesn't mean you have to use just one print. While the two light prints look identical from a distance, closer inspection reveals them to feature different patterns. It's these kinds of subtle surprises that lend texture and vibrancy to a quilt.

making the blocks

Press all seam allowances open to reduce bulk.

1 Trace the trapezoid pattern on page 19 onto template plastic. Cut out the template on the traced lines.

2 Making sure each 2½"-wide strip is right side facing up, use the template to cut 288 shapes from the dark strips. Use the template to cut 152 shapes from the light A strips and 136 shapes from the light B strips.

3 Sew a dark shape to a light A shape to make an A unit. Make 152 units that measure 2½" × 4½", including seam allowances.

Unit A.
Make 152 units,
2½" × 4½".

4 Sew a dark shape to a light B shape to make a B unit. Make 136 units that measure 2½" × 4½", including seam allowances.

Unit B.
Make 136 units,
2½" × 4½".

5 Join two A units to make an A block. Make 40 blocks that measure 4½" square, including seam allowances.

Block A.
Make 40 blocks,
4½" × 4½".

Designed and pieced by Lisa Bongean.

Quilted by Maggi Honeyman.

6 Join two B units to make a B block. Make 32 blocks that measure 4½" square, including seam allowances.

Block B.
Make 32 blocks,
4½" × 4½".

7 Join one A and one B unit to make a C block. Make 72 blocks that measure 4½" square, including seam allowances.

Block C.
Make 72 blocks,
4½" × 4½".

assembling the quilt top

1 Lay out the blocks in 12 rows of 12 blocks each, rotating the blocks as shown in the quilt assembly diagram. Notice that the blocks in rows 1, 5, 8, and 12 are arranged in the same order. The blocks in rows 2, 6, 7, and 11 are arranged in the same order. The blocks in rows 3 and 10 are arranged in the same order. And the blocks in rows 4 and 9 are arranged in the same order.

2 Sew the blocks together into rows. Join the rows. The quilt top should measure 48½" square. Stitch around the perimeter of the quilt top, ⅛" from the outer edges, to lock the seams in place.

finishing the quilt

For more details about any finishing steps, visit ShopMartingale.com/HowtoQuilt.

1 Layer the quilt top, batting, and backing. Hand or machine quilt. What's the Commotion is quilted in an allover fan design.

2 Use the maroon 2¼"-wide strips to make the binding; attach it to the quilt.

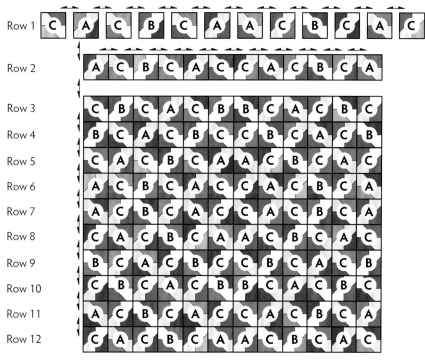

Quilt assembly

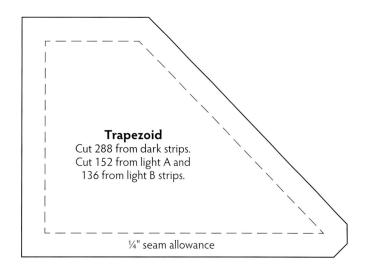

Trapezoid
Cut 288 from dark strips.
Cut 152 from light A and
136 from light B strips.

¼" seam allowance

one-roll wonder

BY BARBARA GROVES AND MARY JACOBSON

Fast, fun, and fabric friendly! What more could you want from a quilt pattern? Me and My Sister Designs, known for their simple-to-piece creations, show off a Jelly Roll in a unique pattern. Love all the fabrics in the Roll? Give them a place to shine on a fabulous throw with 6" bars lined up side by side.

FINISHED QUILT: 60½" × 80½"
FINISHED BLOCK: 10" × 10"

materials

Yardage is based on 42"-wide fabric. Jelly Rolls contain 40 strips, 2½" × width of fabric.

1 Jelly Roll of assorted prints for blocks

2 yards of white solid for blocks

⅝ yard of red check for binding

5 yards of fabric for backing

69" × 89" piece of batting

cutting

From *each* of the assorted print strips, cut:
6 rectangles, 2½" × 6½" (240 total)

From the white solid, cut:
6 strips, 10½" × 42"; crosscut into 96 rectangles,
  2½" × 10½"

From the red check, cut:
8 strips, 2¼" × 42"

making the blocks

Press all seam allowances in the direction indicated by the arrows.

1 Join five print rectangles along their long edges to make a strip unit. Make 48 units that measure 6½" × 10½", including seam allowances.

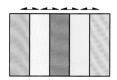

Make 48 units,
6½" × 10½".

2 Sew white rectangles to both long sides of a strip unit to make a block. Make 48 blocks that measure 10½" square, including seam allowances.

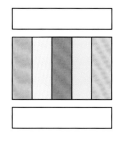 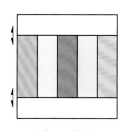

Make 48 blocks,
10½" × 10½".

*Designed and pieced
by Barbara Groves
and Mary Jacobson.*

*Quilted by
Sharon Elsberry.*

assembling the quilt top

1 Lay out the blocks in eight rows of six blocks each, rotating the blocks in each row and from row to row as shown in the quilt assembly diagram on page 23. Sew the blocks together into rows. Join the rows. The quilt top should measure 60½" × 80½".

as shown in the quilt assembly diagram on page 23.

measuring strips

Always measure your Jelly Roll strips from
the outermost tip of the pinked edge.
It's the way to roll if you want accurate
cutting and seam allowances.

2 Stitch around the perimeter of the quilt top, ⅛" from the outer edges, to lock the seams in place.

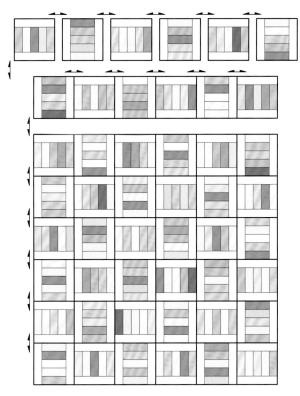

Quilt assembly

finishing the quilt

For more details about any finishing steps, visit ShopMartingale.com/HowtoQuilt.

1 Layer the quilt top, batting, and backing. Hand or machine quilt. One-Roll Wonder is quilted with wavy lines in half of the blocks and a diamond pattern in the remaining blocks. A floral motif is quilted over the block intersections, with swirls between the floral motifs.

2 Use the red 2¼"-wide strips to make the binding; attach it to the quilt.

ROLLIN' WITH
Barbara Groves & Mary Jacobson

If you've ever been somewhere that Barb Groves and Mary Jacobson (MeandMySisterDesigns.com) are, you know they have people rolling in the aisles with laughter. This sister duo likes to keep a little intrigue in their sewing, so you'll have to guess which sister gave which answers.

When I'm sewing with a Jelly Roll, this is how I roll: In pajama pants with a comfy well-worn shirt, a Starbucks tea, and a bag of chocolate-covered peanuts. Heaven! And as for the fabric strips, I use them off the roll just as they are.

My favorite roll is a warm, soft dinner roll with lots of melty butter.

In my dreams, the car I roll up the driveway in is a Lexus convertible.

When I'm on a roll in my sewing room, I order dinner to go, don't shower before bed, and push to the finish line late into the night if needed.

Don't roll your eyes, but I don't change my sewing-machine needle very often. I've also been known to dust the floor around the sewing machine with my sock.

If I'm rolling up my sleeves and getting ready for some serious sewing time, I make sure to find the perfect trashy, mindless reality TV show to binge watch and prewind at least 10 bobbins.

If I could roll back the clock, here's the advice I'd give my younger self: Don't sweat the small stuff and don't worry about cleaning the house before sitting down to sew.

Roll call for my "Sewing Must-Haves" would include these three things: Comfy pants, a sharp rotary cutter, lots of filled bobbins. Did I say comfy pants?

square dance

BY KARLA EISENACH

*Windowpanes, crosshatching, garden lattice—it's the repetition
of shapes that catches the eye. A soft-and-subtle Sweetwater
throw is oh-so-interesting in just the same way.*

FINISHED QUILT: 58" × 58"
FINISHED BLOCK: 12" × 12"

materials

*Yardage is based on 42"-wide fabric. Jelly Rolls contain
40 strips, 2½" × width of fabric.*

1 Jelly Roll of assorted red and tan prints for blocks

1⅛ yards of cream solid for blocks

⅞ yard of tan check for border

¼ yard of cream print for cornerstones

½ yard of red print for binding

3⅝ yards of fabric for backing

64" × 64" piece of batting

cutting

From *each* of 16 red print strips, cut:
4 rectangles, 2½" × 4½" (A; 64 total)
2 squares, 2½" × 2½" (C; 32 total)

From *each* of 16 tan print strips, cut:
4 rectangles, 2½" × 4½" (B; 64 total)
2 squares, 2½" × 2½" (D; 32 total)

From the cream solid, cut:
8 strips, 4½" × 42"; crosscut into 64 squares,
    4½" × 4½" (E)

From the tan check, cut:
5 strips, 5¼" × 42"

From the cream print, cut:
4 squares, 5¼" × 5¼"

From the red print for binding, cut:
7 strips, 2¼" × 42"

making the blocks

Press all seam allowances in the direction indicated by
the arrows.

1 Lay out two matching A rectangles, one C square,
and one E square as shown. Sew the squares and
rectangles together into rows. Join the rows to make a
red unit. Make 32 units that measure 6½" square,
including seam allowances.

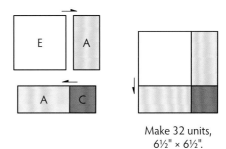

Make 32 units,
6½" × 6½".

2 In the same way, join two matching B rectangles,
one D square, and one E square to make a tan unit.
Make 32 units that measure 6½" square, including
seam allowances.

Make 32 units,
6½" × 6½".

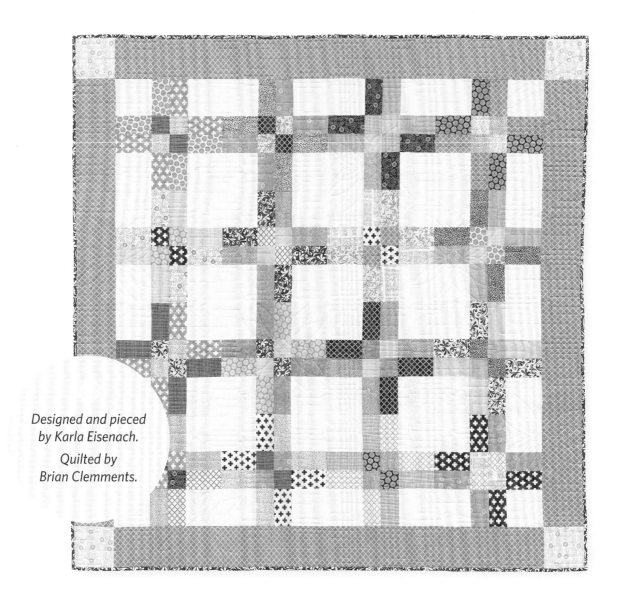

*Designed and pieced
by Karla Eisenach.
Quilted by
Brian Clemments.*

3 Arrange two matching red units and two matching tan units in two rows, rotating the units as shown. Sew the units together into rows. Join the rows to make a block. Make 16 blocks that measure 12½" square, including seam allowances.

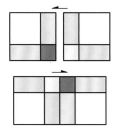

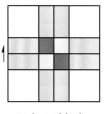

Make 16 blocks,
12½" × 12½".

assembling the quilt top

1 Lay out the blocks in four rows of four blocks each as shown in the quilt assembly diagram on page 27. Sew the blocks together into rows. Join the rows to make the quilt-top center, which should measure 48½" square, including seam allowances.

2 Join the tan check strips end to end to make a long strip. From the pieced strip, cut four 48½"-long strips. Sew two of these strips to opposite sides of the quilt-top center.

3 Sew a cream print square to the ends of each remaining tan check strip as shown in the quilt assembly diagram. Sew these strips to the top and bottom of the quilt top. The quilt top should measure 58" square.

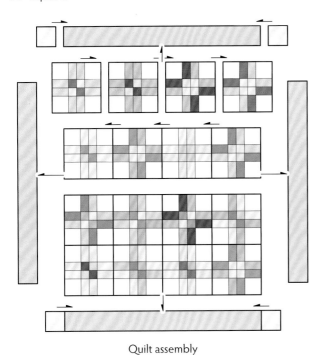

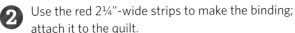

Quilt assembly

finishing the quilt

For more details about any finishing steps, visit ShopMartingale.com/HowtoQuilt.

1 Layer the quilt top, batting, and backing. Hand or machine quilt. Square Dance is quilted with an allover pattern that combines straight lines and a floral motif.

2 Use the red 2¼"-wide strips to make the binding; attach it to the quilt.

ROLLIN' WITH
Karla Eisenach

If you were rolling in dough with designer Karla Eisenach (TheSweetWaterCo.com), it'd have to be for a sweet roll! Cinnamon? Orange? Who knows? One thing is for certain. Her quilt design skills are S–WEET!

When I'm sewing with a Jelly Roll, this is how I roll: If a quilt is scrappy, I first cut the strips into pieces according to the pattern. After that, I pair each piece with a coordinating one before sewing, so that I'm not left with all the same prints for the last few blocks or units.

My favorite rolls are Parker House rolls from a cookbook recipe that I've had for 45 years.

In my dreams, the car I roll up the driveway in is new. My car is 11 years old, so anything new would be a dream!

When I'm on a roll in my sewing room, I just want to finish a new project without interruptions.

Don't roll your eyes, but I often start a new project before finishing the previous one. Doesn't everybody do that?

If I'm rolling up my sleeves and getting ready for some serious sewing time, I make sure to eat and have snacks ready!

If I could roll back the clock, here's the advice I'd give my younger self: Don't be afraid to try something new.

Roll call for my "Sewing Must-Haves" would include these three things: A sharp rotary-cutter blade, small scissors close by, and Netflix.

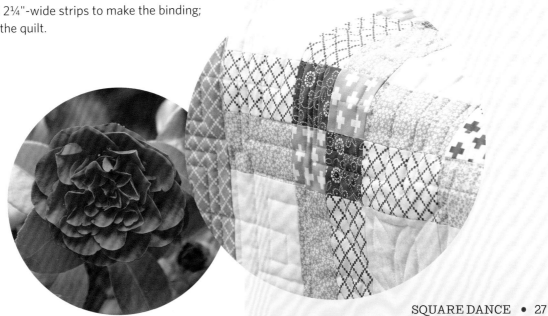

pineapple quilt

BY BRIGITTE HEITLAND

A classic pineapple design mixes light prints and colorful solids. Starting with 2½"-wide strips reduces the cutting time and speeds up the block sewing, leaving you more time to admire your quilt!

FINISHED QUILT: 60½" × 60½"
FINISHED BLOCK: 20" × 20"

materials

Yardage is based on 42"-wide fabric. Jelly Rolls contain 40 strips, 2½" × width of fabric.

1 Jelly Roll of assorted bright solids for blocks

1 Jelly Roll of assorted light prints for blocks

⅞ yard of orange solid for blocks

½ yard of gray solid for binding

3¾ yards of fabric for backing

67" × 67" piece of batting

cutting

From the assorted bright solid strips, cut a *total* of:
36 rectangles, 2½" × 9½" (H)
36 rectangles, 2½" × 8" (F)
36 rectangles, 2½" × 6¼" (D)
36 rectangles, 2½" × 4½" (B)

From the orange solid, cut:
3 strips, 5½" × 42"; crosscut into 18 squares, 5½" × 5½".
   Cut the squares in half diagonally to yield 36 triangles (J).
2 strips, 4½" × 42"; crosscut into 9 squares, 4½" × 4½" (A)

From the assorted light print strips, cut a *total* of:
36 rectangles, 2½" × 11¼" (I)
36 rectangles, 2½" × 9¾" (G)
36 rectangles, 2½" × 8" (E)
36 rectangles, 2½" × 6¼" (C)

From the gray solid, cut:
7 strips, 2¼" × 42"

making the blocks

After sewing each seam, press the seam allowances toward the just-added rectangle.

1 Sew B rectangles to opposite sides of an A square. Sew B rectangles to remaining sides of the square. Make nine units.

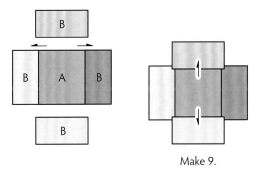

Make 9.

2 Place a unit *wrong* side up on a cutting mat. Align a 45° line on an acrylic ruler with the corners of the center square. Then place the ruler's long edge ¼" beyond the seam intersection. Use a rotary cutter to trim along the edge of the ruler. Repeat to trim the remaining corners of the B rectangles. Trim each A/B unit in the same way.

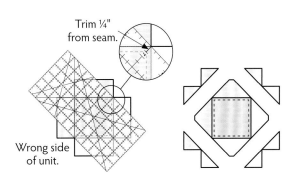

Trim ¼" from seam.

Wrong side of unit.

Designed and pieced by Brigitte Heitland.

Quilted by Carrie Straka of Red Velvet Quilts.

3 Sew C rectangles to opposite sides of an A/B unit. Sew C rectangles to the remaining sides of the unit. Make nine units. Repeat step 2 to trim the C rectangles on each unit. The units should measure 8½" square, including seam allowances.

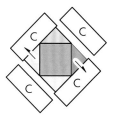

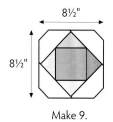

Make 9.

4 Sew D rectangles to the trimmed edges of a unit from step 3. Make nine units.

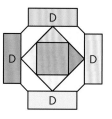

Make 9.

5 Place a unit from step 4 *wrong* side up on a cutting mat. Align a 45° line on an acrylic ruler with the corners of the center square (or any other diagonal seamline). Align the ruler's long edge with the edges of the C rectangle. The edge of the ruler should be 2¼" from the stitching line as shown. Use a rotary cutter to trim along the edge of the ruler. Repeat to trim the remaining corners of the D rectangles. The unit should measure 12½" square, including seam allowances. Trim each unit in the same way.

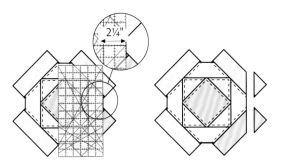

6 Referring to the block diagram on page 32 for color placement, add each set of the remaining rectangles from E through H. Repeat step 5 to trim the rectangles 2¼" from the previous stitching line. After adding each set of rectangles, measure the units to make sure they are the correct size. After adding the E rectangles, the units should measure 12½" square, including seam allowances. After adding the G rectangles, they should measure 16½" square, including seam allowances. After adding the H rectangles, they should measure 20½" square, including seam allowances.

ROLLIN' WITH
Brigitte Heitland

Let the good times roll with an aesthetic that's a little bit modern, always artful, and fun to piece. That's what you get when designer Brigitte Heitland of Zen Chic (BrigitteHeitland.de) has her sewing-machine pedal to the metal!

When I'm sewing with a Jelly Roll, this is how I roll: First I have a pattern idea in mind and choose a Jelly Roll of a collection that serves the pattern idea. If the pattern has a scrappy look, I pick totally randomly from my Jelly Roll, adjusting piecing combinations as I go if the random selections wouldn't make for a good fit.

My favorite roll is a *Schneckennudel*. Translated literally from German, *Schneckennudel* means "snail noodle." It comes with raisins, a hint of cinnamon, and sugar icing.

In my dreams, the car I roll up the driveway in is a red Alfa Romeo Spider Cabriolet, '70s style.

When I'm on a roll in my sewing room, I am in my flow. I listen to dance music or a good audio book, forget all stress and worries, and enjoy the noise of my sewing machine and the warmth of my ironing process.

Don't roll your eyes, but I often gather little 1½" squares to feed them through my machine during the chain-sewing process. I make ribbons out of the little squares, which I later stitch on towels.

If I'm rolling up my sleeves and getting ready for some serious sewing time, I make sure to have all pieces cut in advance and nicely organized on my sewing table.

If I could roll back the clock, here's the advice I'd give my younger self: Be patient—things will work out in time, and often better than expected.

Roll call for my "Sewing Must-Haves" would include these three things: A nicely organized case for all my sewing supplies, a good audio book, and a weekend off.

7 Add the I rectangles. Repeat step 5 to trim the rectangles. Then add the J triangles to make a Pineapple block. Make nine blocks that measure 20½" square, including seam allowances.

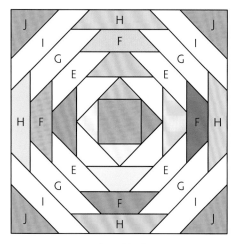

Make 9 blocks,
20½" × 20½".

assembling the quilt top

Press all seam allowances in the direction indicated by the arrows.

1 Lay out blocks in three rows of three blocks each as shown in the quilt assembly diagram below. Sew the blocks together into rows. Join the rows. The quilt top should measure 60½" square.

2 Stitch around the perimeter of the quilt top, ⅛" from the outer edges, to lock the seams in place.

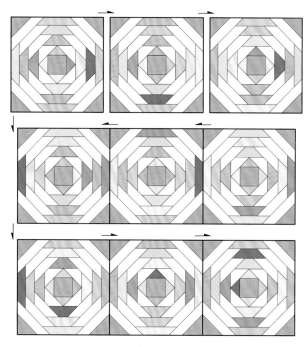

Quilt assembly

finishing the quilt

For more details about any finishing steps, visit ShopMartingale.com/HowtoQuilt.

1 Layer the quilt top, batting, and backing. Hand or machine quilt. Pineapple Quilt is quilted with straight lines in a grid pattern.

2 Use the gray 2¼"-wide strips to make the binding; attach it to the quilt.

sweet butterfly

BY STACY IEST HSU

Like a caterpillar transforming into a beautiful butterfly, a Jelly Roll turns into a garden of colorful flutter-byes. Sort your strips by color or mix and match to make one-of-a-kind colorations. It might be your nature to have no two alike!

FINISHED QUILT: 63" × 68½"
FINISHED BLOCK: 17½" × 14"

materials

Yardage is based on 42"-wide fabric. Jelly Rolls contain 40 strips, 2½" × width of fabric.

1 Jelly Roll of assorted aqua, pink, yellow, green, and cream prints for blocks*

2⅞ yards of white solid for blocks, sashing, and border

⅝ yard of pink dot for blocks and binding

¼ yard of aqua dot for blocks

⅛ yard of green dot for blocks

⅛ yard of yellow dot for blocks

3⅞ yards of fabric for backing

69" × 75" piece of batting

The pink and aqua strips need to range in value from light to dark. The strips with a dark or medium background are referred to as "dark pink" and "dark aqua." The strips with a lighter background are referred to as "light pink" and "light aqua." All strips with a cream background are collectively referred to as "cream."

cutting

From the white solid, cut:
25 strips, 2½" × 42"; crosscut *20 strips* into:
    8 strips, 2½" × 14½"
    24 rectangles, 2½" × 6½"
    192 squares, 2½" × 2½"
7 strips, 3½" × 42"
1 strip, 2" × 42"; crosscut into 12 rectangles, 2" × 2½"
2 strips, 1" × 42"; crosscut into 48 squares, 1" × 1"

From the pink dot, cut:
7 strips, 2¼" × 42"
2 strips, 2" × 42"; crosscut into 4 strips, 2" × 12½"

From the dark pink strips and remaining pink dot, cut a *total* of:
6 rectangles, 2½" × 8½"
6 rectangles, 2½" × 6½"
6 squares, 2½" × 2½"
6 squares, 1½" × 1½"

From the aqua dot, cut:
2 strips, 2" × 42"; crosscut into 4 strips, 2" × 12½"

From the dark aqua strips and remaining aqua dot, cut a *total* of:
6 rectangles, 2½" × 8½"
6 rectangles, 2½" × 6½"
6 squares, 2½" × 2½"
6 squares, 1½" × 1½"

From the green dot, cut:
1 strip, 2" × 42"; crosscut into 2 strips, 2" × 12½"

Continued on page 35

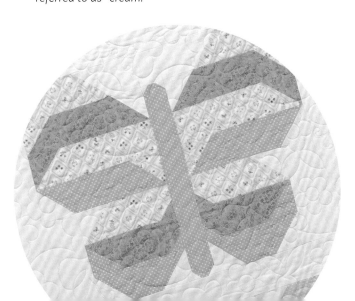

Continued from page 33

From the yellow dot, cut:

1 strip, 2" × 42"; crosscut into 2 strips, 2" × 12½"

From the light pink strips, cut a *total* of:

12 rectangles, 2½" × 8½"

18 rectangles, 2½" × 6½"

20 squares, 2½" × 2½"

8 squares, 1½" × 1½"

From the light aqua strips, cut a *total* of:

10 rectangles, 2½" × 8½"

10 rectangles, 2½" × 6½"

16 squares, 2½" × 2½"

10 squares, 1½" × 1½"

From the green strips, cut a *total* of:

10 rectangles, 2½" × 8½"

10 rectangles, 2½" × 6½"

12 squares, 2½" × 2½"

6 squares, 1½" × 1½"

From the yellow strips, cut a *total* of:

6 rectangles, 2½" × 8½"

12 rectangles, 2½" × 6½"

8 squares, 2½" × 2½"

4 squares, 1½" × 1½"

From the cream strips, cut a *total* of:

22 rectangles, 2½" × 8½"

34 rectangles, 2½" × 6½"

28 squares, 2½" × 2½"

8 squares, 1½" × 1½"

making the units

Refer to the photo on page 33 for placement guidance. Each block is constructed using the fabrics from one color family. Directions are for making one of the pink blocks. Repeat the steps to make a total of four pink, four aqua, two green, and two yellow blocks (12 total). Although the construction is the same for each block, the placement of the light, dark, and cream prints varies from block to block. Some blocks are made using light and cream prints. Press all seam allowances in the direction indicated by the arrows.

1 Draw a diagonal line from corner to corner on the wrong side of four white 2½" squares. Place marked squares on each end of a light pink 2½" × 6½" rectangle, right sides together, making sure to orient the

marked lines as shown. Sew on the marked lines. Trim the excess corner fabric, ¼" from the stitched line. Make two units that measure 2½" × 6½", including seam allowances.

Make 2 units, 2½" × 6½".

2 Sew a white 2½" square to the right end of a unit from step 1 to make an A unit. Sew a white 2½" square to the left end of a unit from step 1 to make a reversed A unit. The units should now measure 2½" × 8½", including seam allowances.

Make 1 of each unit, 2½" × 8½".

3 Draw a diagonal line on the wrong side of two white and two light pink 2½" squares that match the A units. Place a light pink square on the left end of a dark pink 2½" × 8½" rectangle, right sides together, making sure to orient the square as shown. Sew on the marked line. Trim the excess corner fabric, ¼" from the stitched line. Place a white square on the right end of the dark pink rectangle. Sew and trim to make a B unit. Repeat to make a reversed B unit. The units should measure 2½" × 8½", including seam allowances.

Make 1 of each unit, 2½" × 8½".

4 Draw a diagonal line on the wrong side of two dark pink 2½" squares that match the B units. Place a marked square on the left end of a light pink 2½" × 8½" rectangle, right sides together. Sew on the marked line. Trim the excess corner fabric, ¼" from the stitched line. Make one C unit and one reversed C unit. The units should measure 2½" × 8½", including seam allowances.

Make 1 of each unit, 2½" × 8½".

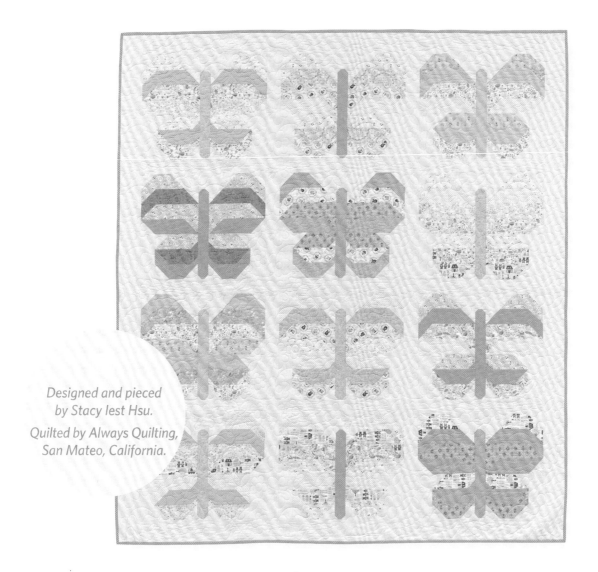

5 Draw a diagonal line on the wrong side of two white and two light pink 2½" squares. The light pink squares should match the C units. Place a white square on the left end and a light pink square on the right end of a dark pink or pink dot 2½" × 8½" rectangle, right sides together, making sure to orient the squares as shown. Sew on the marked lines. Trim the excess corner fabric, ¼" from the stitched line, to make a D unit. Repeat to make a reversed D unit. The units should measure 2½" × 8½", including seam allowances.

 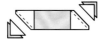

Make 1 of each unit, 2½" × 8½".

6 Draw a diagonal line on the wrong side of two white 2½" squares and two dark pink 1½" squares. The dark pink squares should match the F rectangle. Place a white square on the left end of a light pink 2½" × 6½" rectangle, right sides together, making sure to orient the square as shown. Sew on the marked line. Trim the excess corner fabric, ¼" from the stitched line. Place a dark pink square on the lower-right corner of the light pink rectangle. Sew and trim to make an E unit. Repeat to make a reversed E unit. The units should measure 2½" × 6½", including seam allowances.

Make 1 of each unit, 2½" × 6½".

7 Draw a diagonal line on the wrong side of two dark pink or pink dot 2½" squares and two dark pink or pink dot 1½" squares. The squares should match the D unit. Place a 2½" square on the left end of a dark pink 2½" × 6½" rectangle, right sides together, making sure to orient the square as shown. The rectangle should match the B units. Sew on the marked line. Trim the excess corner fabric, ¼" from the stitched line. Place a 1½" square on the lower-right corner of the dark pink rectangle. Sew and trim to make an F unit. Repeat to make a reversed F unit. The units should measure 2½" × 6½", including seam allowances.

Make 1 of each unit, 2½" × 6½".

8 Draw a diagonal line on the wrong side of four white 2½" squares. Place marked squares on each end of a dark pink or pink dot 2½" × 6½" rectangle, right sides together, making sure to orient the marked lines as shown. The rectangle should match the D units. Sew on the marked lines. Trim the excess corner fabric, ¼" from the stitched line. Make two G units that measure 2½" × 6½", including seam allowances.

Make 2 units, 2½" × 6½".

check before trimming

Before trimming the excess corner fabric, flip the square back over the corner, right side facing up, and check for accuracy. Be careful not to stretch the square. It should lie exactly on the corner of the rectangle. If the resulting triangle is too small, resew the seam. If the edges of the square extend beyond the rectangle, you can trim the unit to size.

9 Draw a diagonal line from corner to corner on the wrong side of four white 1" squares. Place a marked square on one corner of a pink dot 2" × 12½" strip. Sew on the marked line. Trim the excess corner fabric, ¼" from the stitched line. Repeat to sew marked squares on the remaining corners of the pink dot strip. Make one unit that measures 2" × 12½", including seam allowances.

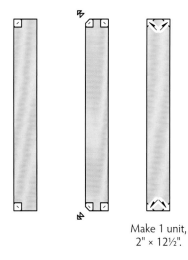

Make 1 unit,
2" × 12½".

10 Sew a white 2" × 2½" rectangle to the top of the unit from step 9 to make a center unit that measures 2" × 14½", including seam allowances.

Make 1 unit,
2" × 14½".

assembling the block

① Join units A, B, C, and D as shown to make the upper-left wing unit. Join reversed A, B, C, and D units to make the upper-right wing unit. The units should measure 8½" square, including seam allowances.

Make 1 of each unit,
8½" × 8½".

② Join units E, F, and G as shown. Then sew a white 2½" × 6½" rectangle to the left side of the unit to make the lower-left wing unit. Join reversed E and F units and the remaining G unit. Sew a white 2½" × 6½" rectangle to the right side of the reversed unit to make the lower-right wing unit. The units should measure 6½" × 8½", including seam allowances.

Make 1 of each unit,
6½" × 8½".

③ Lay out the upper wing units, lower wing units, and the center unit as shown. Join the upper and lower wing units to make the right and left wings. Join the wings to the center unit to make a block that measures 18" × 14½", including the seam allowances.

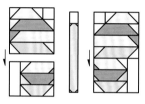 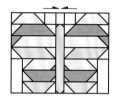

Make 1 block,
18" × 14½".

④ Repeat all steps to make a total of four pink, four aqua, two green, and two yellow blocks (12 total).

assembling the quilt top

① Join three blocks and two white 2½" × 14½" strips to make a block row. Repeat to make a total of four block rows that measure 14½" × 57", including seam allowances.

② Join the five remaining white 2½"-wide strips end to end. From the pieced strip, cut three 57"-long sashing strips.

③ Sew the block rows and long sashing strips together as shown in the quilt assembly diagram on page 39. The quilt-top center should measure 57" × 62½", including seam allowances.

4 Join the white 3½"-wide strips end to end. From the pieced strip, cut two 68½"-long strips and two 57"-long strips. Sew the 57"-long strips to the top and bottom of the quilt top. Sew the 68½"-long strips to opposite sides of the quilt top. The quilt top should measure 63" × 68½".

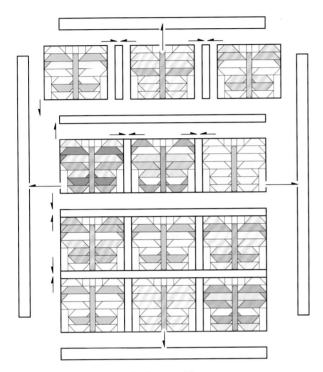

Quilt assembly

finishing the quilt

For more details about any finishing steps, visit ShopMartingale.com/HowtoQuilt.

1 Layer the quilt top, batting, and backing. Hand or machine quilt. Sweet Butterfly is quilted with an allover pattern of butterflies, flowers, leaves, and loops.

2 Use the pink dot 2¼"-wide strips to make the binding; attach it to the quilt.

ROLLIN' WITH
Stacy Iest Hsu

As a busy mom and designer, Stacy (StacyIestHsu.com) has learned to roll with the punches. Her to-do list is full, but she's always ready to make time for her design work. So happy to hear that!

When I'm sewing with a Jelly Roll, this is how I roll: The first thing I do is unroll and sort by color to see what I have to work with. I then press and trim the selvages and get to work on placing the pieces.

My favorite roll is a Sourdough roll. Come on, I'm from the Bay Area! It's really the only answer for me, right?

In my dreams, the car I roll up the driveway in is a car service. I hate driving.

When I'm on a roll in my sewing room, I pretty much power through without checking emails and messages. I do manage to pick up the kids, but oftentimes I will bring my project in the car to work on while I wait for them.

Don't roll your eyes, but I don't clean my sewing machine as much as I should.

If I'm rolling up my sleeves and getting ready for some serious sewing time, I make sure to turn on the Food Network and get to work. This way I can multitask: sew and get ideas for dinner.

If I could roll back the clock, here's the advice I'd give my younger self: Do not compare yourself to what other people are doing, either career-wise or life-wise.

Roll call for my "Sewing Must-Haves" would include these three things: A cup of coffee, a new rotary-cutter blade, and a seam ripper.

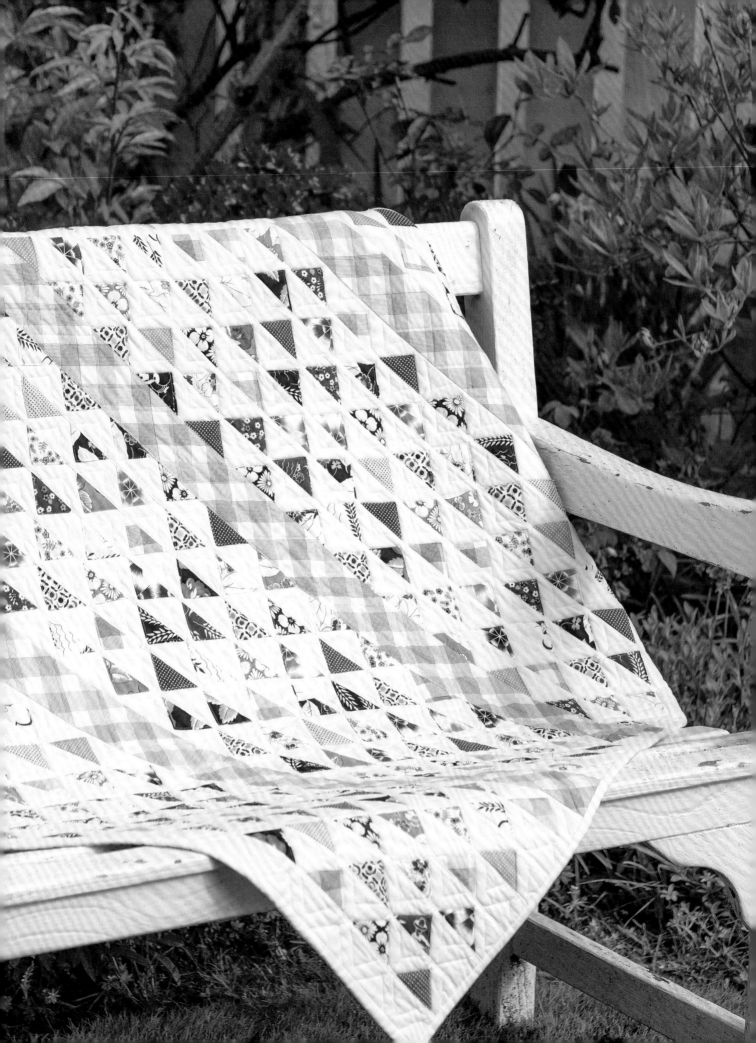

on the flip side

BY PAM EHRHARDT AND LINZEE MCCRAY

Let's get to the point here . . . the prairie point, that is! What do you see when you look at this quilt? White triangles with a blue background, or blue triangles with a white background? Whichever stands out to you, check "adorable" on your list! And let's get to sewing.

FINISHED QUILT: 44" × 44"

materials

Yardage is based on 42"-wide fabric. Jelly Rolls contain 40 strips, 2½" × width of fabric.

1 Jelly Roll of assorted blue prints for folded triangles

2¾ yards of white solid for background and binding

⅜ yard of blue diagonal check for sashing strips

2⅞ yards of fabric for backing*

50" × 50" piece of batting

*If you want to use the leftover Jelly Roll strips to piece the backing, see "Make a Pieced Backing" on page 45. If you piece the backing and your fabric is at least 42" wide after removing the selvages, you will need 1½ yards of fabric.

cutting

From *each* of 29 assorted blue strips, cut:
16 squares, 2½" × 2½" (464 total)

From the white solid, cut on the *lengthwise* grain:
2 strips, 40" × 44"; crosscut into:
    5 strips, 2¼" × 44"
    30 strips, 1¾" × 44"

From the blue diagonal check, cut:
4 strips, 2½" × 42"

making the folded triangles

1 Fold a blue square in half diagonally, wrong sides together, being careful to match the raw edges. Press. Fold again, matching corners carefully, and press. Make 464 folded triangles.

Two folds

Make 464.

2 Machine baste ⅛" from the raw edges of each folded triangle. This will help hold the triangles closed when they are sewn to the background strips.

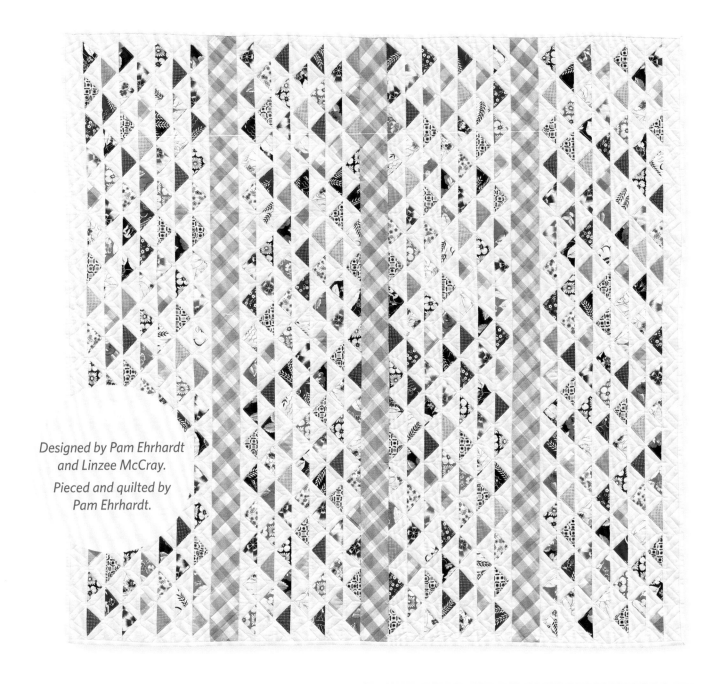

Designed by Pam Ehrhardt and Linzee McCray.

Pieced and quilted by Pam Ehrhardt.

Arranging the Triangles

When attaching the triangles to the background strips, you can arrange them randomly or place them deliberately with regard to color and pattern. If you choose to do the latter, it's helpful to lay the adjacent strips nearby as you sew, checking for placement of colors and patterns. You may also want to label these strips to keep them in order, for example A–1, B–2, A–3, B–4, and so on.

making the strip units

Refer to the illustrations below for all four steps.

1 On a white 1¾"-wide strip, measure ¾" from each end and make a small mark (about ⅛" long) in the seam allowance. Measure 2½" from the mark on one end and make a small mark. Continue to make small marks 2½" apart as shown until you have a total of 18 marks. Repeat to make a total of 16 marked strips and label them as A strips.

2 On a white 1¾"-wide strip, measure 2" from each end and make a small mark (about ⅛" long) in the seam allowance. Measure 2½" from the mark on one end and make a small mark. Continue to make small marks 2½" apart until you have a total of 17 marks. Repeat to make a total of 12 marked strips and label them as B strips.

3 On a marked A strip, center and pin a triangle between two 2½" marks, aligning the raw edges of the triangle with the raw edge of the strip. In the same way, position 17 folded triangles along the marked edge of the strip. Machine baste the triangles in place, stitching ⅛" from the edges. Make 16.

4 On a marked B strip, position and machine baste 16 folded triangles along the marked edge of the strip as you did in step 3. Make 12.

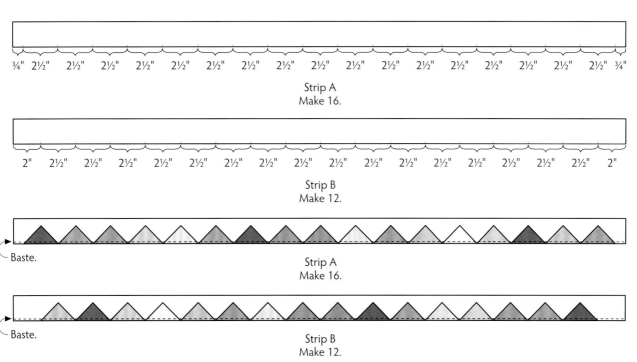

¾" 2½" 2½" 2½" 2½" 2½" 2½" 2½" 2½" 2½" 2½" 2½" 2½" 2½" 2½" 2½" 2½" 2½" ¾"

Strip A
Make 16.

2" 2½" 2½" 2½" 2½" 2½" 2½" 2½" 2½" 2½" 2½" 2½" 2½" 2½" 2½" 2½" 2½" 2"

Strip B
Make 12.

Baste.

Strip A
Make 16.

Baste.

Strip B
Make 12.

assembling the quilt top

Press all seam allowances in the direction indicated by the arrows.

1 Lay out four A strips and three B strips, alternating them and making sure the triangles are all pointing in the same direction. Join the strips to make a column. Make four columns that measure 9¼" × 44", including seam allowances.

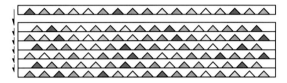

Make 4 columns,
9¼" × 44".

2 Join the blue check strips end to end. From the pieced strip, cut three 44"-long strips.

3 Lay out the two remaining white 1¾"-wide strips, the four columns, and the three blue check strips, rotating two of the columns as shown in the quilt assembly diagram below. Join the strips and columns to make the quilt top, which should measure 44" square, including seam allowances. Stitch around the top and bottom of the quilt top, ⅛" from the outer edges, to lock the seams in place.

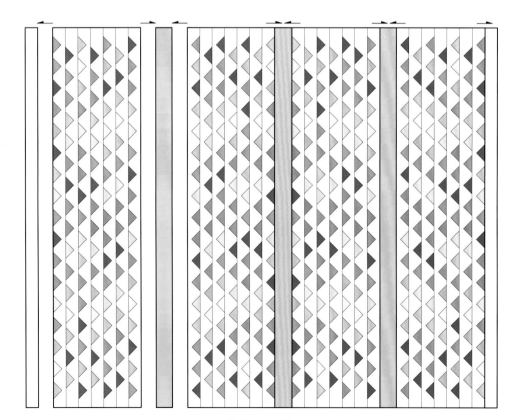

Quilt assembly

Make a Pieced Backing

You can use the leftover 2½"-wide strips to make a pieced backing.

1. Cut six of the remaining Jelly Roll strips into random lengths.

2. Join the lengths end to end to make one long strip, alternating the prints. Press the seam allowances open. From the pieced strip, cut four 50"-long strips.

3. Cut the pressed backing fabric lengthwise to make two pieces: one 14" × 50" and one 28" × 50" piece.

4. Sew the pieced strips together to make a section that measures 8½" × 50", including seam allowances.

5. Sew the pieced section between the two pieces of backing. The backing should be 49½" × 50".

finishing the quilt

For more details about any finishing steps, visit ShopMartingale.com/HowtoQuilt.

1 Layer the quilt top, batting, and backing. Hand or machine quilt. On the Flip Side is quilted on top of each triangle, along the folded edge, to secure the triangle points to the background. Zigzag lines are quilted in the background, side borders, and sashing strips.

2 Use the white 2¼"-wide strips to make the binding; attach it to the quilt.

ROLLIN' WITH
Linzee McCray

Linzee (LinzeeKullMcCray.com) is likely to roll out the red carpet for you if you're a vintage-feedsack lover like she is! An author, designer, and writer, her fabrics with Moda are inspired by feedsack prints.

When I'm sewing with a Jelly Roll, this is how I roll: I'm a fan of random—I love mixing up strips, although I'm not above a little "adjusting" if I think it would improve the overall look.

My favorite roll is my Aunt Marcia's sweet rolls. She was renowned for her caramel-and-nut covered breakfast treats, and she'd bake them whenever we'd visit her farm. She shared the recipe and we all tried our hand at making them, but none were as good as hers. She definitely had the magic touch.

When I'm on a roll in my sewing room, I queue a bunch of podcasts so I can just keep listening and not stop sewing. I love everything from sewing shows and celebrity interviews to political and economic podcasts. There's so much choice!

Don't roll your eyes, but I often forget to have my sewing machine serviced regularly. And boy, when I do have it serviced, I can really tell the difference!

If I'm rolling up my sleeves and getting ready for some serious sewing time, I make sure to announce that I won't be cooking that day . . . or that weekend. My husband's great about making meals or ordering pizza.

If I could roll back the clock, here's the advice I'd give my younger self: Be persistent and be willing to change perspective. If someone tells you no about a project, or if a sewing technique doesn't work exactly as written, take a different approach and try again. There are so many ways to accomplish the same thing, and instead of being discouraged if the first way doesn't work, try another! Keep trying!

Roll call for my "Sewing Must-Haves" would include these three things: Curved-tip scissors, which make me feel less nervous about cutting threads close; a chopstick for turning corners on bags and pillows; Aurifil thread in every color I can get my hands on; and That Purple Thang, for a little extra help with holding, pushing, pulling, etc. (That's four, but who's counting!)

trifle

BY JANET CLARE

Trifle, the (slightly eccentric) name for this quilt, popped into the designer's mind (as the best ideas frequently do). If you haven't had the pleasure of eating trifle, it's a British dessert popular at family gatherings, made from sherry-soaked sponge cake, fresh fruit, jelly, custard, and whipped cream, all carefully layered into a glass bowl. The colorful fabric strips in this pattern capture the same layered appeal of that delectable treat.

FINISHED QUILT: 63½" × 63½"
FINISHED BLOCK: 7" × 7"

materials

Yardage is based on 42"-wide fabric. Jelly Rolls contain 40 strips, 2½" × width of fabric.

2 Jelly Rolls of assorted prints for blocks and binding*

81 squares, 5" × 5", of assorted prints for blocks*

4 yards of fabric for backing

70" × 70" piece of batting

Foundation paper

*Janet used 2 Jelly Rolls and 2 charm square packs from the same collection. She used the leftover 2½"-wide strips for binding. If you prefer 2¼"-wide binding, trim the strips to be narrower. If you want to use one fabric for the binding, you'll need ⅝ yard.

making the blocks

Press all seam allowances in the direction indicated by the arrows.

1 From the foundation paper, cut 81 squares, 7½" × 7½". Fold each paper-foundation square in half horizontally and vertically to establish centering lines.

2 Set aside seven of the print strips for the binding. Cut 50 of the remaining print strips lengthwise to make 50 strings that measure 1" × 42" and 50 that measure 1½" × 42". When making blocks, cut additional strings as needed from the remaining print strips.

3 Pin a print 5" square in the center of a paper foundation, right side up, and align the corners of the square with the fold lines.

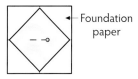

Foundation paper

4 Using a print string of either width, place the string on one side of the square, right sides together. Align one end of the string with the corner of the square. Stitch along the edges of the fabric, using a ¼" seam allowance and sewing through all three layers (string, square, and paper). Press the string open. Trim the string even with the square. Save the remaining string to use for another block.

5 Using a print string of either width, place the string on an adjacent side of the square, right sides together. In the same way as before, stitch along the edges of the fabric. Press the string open. Trim the string even with the square. Save the remaining string to use for another block.

Designed by Janet Clare.
Pieced by Paula Hope.
Quilted by Carolyn Clark.

Create a Cushion!

Having too much fun to stop stitching?
Rather than save your scraps for a future project,
sew them into a coordinating cushion.

6 Repeat step 5 to add a third and then a fourth string to the center square.

7 Continue in the same way, sewing strings to the center unit and using the shorter lengths as you near the corners of the block, until the entire foundation square is covered. Always work in the same direction as the first round of strings (either clockwise or counterclockwise). Make 81 blocks. Trim the blocks to measure 7½" square, including seam allowances.

Make 81 blocks,
7½" × 7½".

assembling the quilt top

1 Lay out the blocks in nine rows of nine blocks each as shown in the quilt assembly diagram below. Sew the blocks together into rows. Join the rows. The quilt top should measure 63½" square.

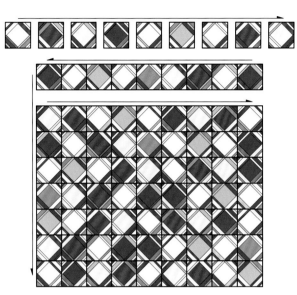

Quilt assembly

2 Stitch around the perimeter of the quilt top, ⅛" from the outer edges, to lock the seams in place. Remove the foundation papers from the blocks.

finishing the quilt

For more details about any finishing steps, visit ShopMartingale.com/HowtoQuilt.

1 Layer the quilt top, batting, and backing. Hand or machine quilt. Trifle is quilted with an allover design of Christmas trees.

2 Use the seven print 2½"-wide strips you set aside in step 2 of "Making the Blocks" to make the binding; attach it to the quilt.

ROLLIN' WITH
Janet Clare

She's ready to roll when you are! Designer Janet Clare (JanetClare.co.uk) likes to be creative every day and doesn't believe in keeping things "for best." So let's get started.

When I'm sewing with a Jelly Roll, this is how I roll: I unroll and admire all the strips, leave them all in a muddle, and go from there.

My favorite roll is a Swiss roll.

In my dreams, the car I roll up the driveway in is a Mini Countryman. It has wooden trim, leather seats, and double doors that open wide at the back.

When I'm on a roll in my sewing room, I have to set an alarm so I remember to go home and feed the family!

Don't roll your eyes, but I often use polyester thread for piecing.

If I'm rolling up my sleeves and getting ready for some serious sewing time, I make sure to microwave some meals, open Netflix, and put the kettle on.

If I could roll back the clock, here's the advice I'd give my younger self: Keep your best clothes—you're going to want those Laura Ashley fabrics later!

Roll call for my "Sewing Must-Haves" would include these three things: An iron, starch, and chocolate.

parfait

BY SHERRI MCCONNELL

Create a happy-go-lucky throw with a fool-the-eye twist. Four matching Shoofly blocks sashed side by side sometimes appear spiky at the corners, and other times you're sure they look more like snowballs. The secret? It's all in the contrast between the strips you choose.

FINISHED QUILT: 64½" × 78½"
FINISHED BLOCK: 13" × 13"

materials

Yardage is based on 42"-wide fabric. Jelly Rolls contain 40 strips, 2½" × width of fabric. Fat eighths measure 9" × 21".

2 Jelly Rolls of assorted prints for blocks*

5 yards of cream solid for blocks, sashing, and inner border

1 fat eighth of pink print for sashing squares

⅞ yard of blue floral for outer border

⅝ yard of pink solid for binding

4¾ yards of fabric for backing

71" × 85" piece of batting

*The Jelly Rolls need to contain 2 matching strips each of 20 dark and 5 light prints.

cutting

From *each* of 40 assorted dark print strips, cut:
2 strips, 2½" × 21" (20 sets of 4 matching strips; 80 total)

From *each* of 10 assorted light print strips, cut:
2 strips, 2½" × 21" (5 sets of 4 matching strips; 20 total; you'll use 3 strips from each set)

From the cream solid, cut:
43 strips, 2½" × 42"; crosscut into:
    45 strips, 2½" × 21"
    320 squares, 2½" × 2½"
27 strips, 1½" × 42"; crosscut into:
    31 rectangles, 1½" × 13½"
    80 rectangles, 1½" × 6½"
7 strips, 2" × 42"

From the pink print, cut:
12 squares, 1½" × 1½"

From the blue floral, cut:
8 strips, 3½" × 42"

From the pink solid, cut:
8 strips, 2¼" × 42"

making the blocks

Each block is made using one dark print and one light print or cream solid. Directions are for making one block. Repeat to make a total of 20 blocks. Press all seam allowances in the direction indicated by the arrows.

1 Join two matching dark strips and one light (or cream) 2½" × 21" strip to make a strip set that measures 6½" × 21", including seam allowances. Crosscut the strip set into eight segments, 2½" × 6½".

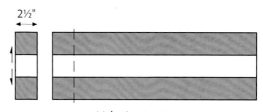

2½"

Make 1 strip set.
Cut 8 segments, 2½" × 6½".

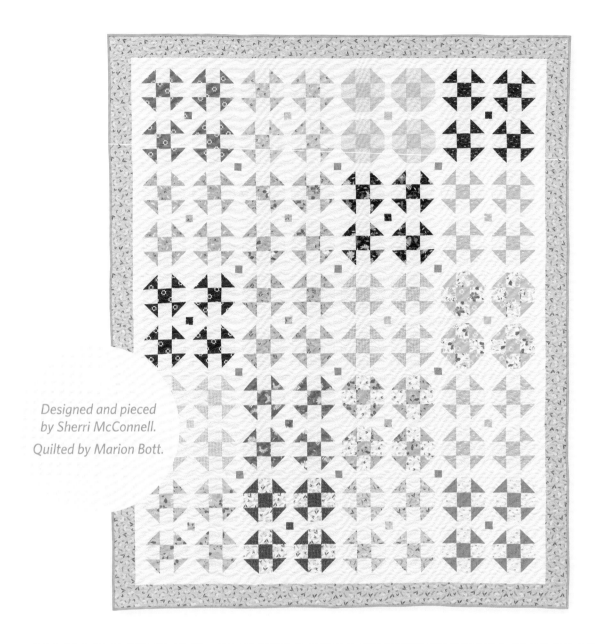

*Designed and pieced
by Sherri McConnell.
Quilted by Marion Bott.*

2 Join two light (or cream) 2½" × 21" strips and one dark strip to make a strip set that measures 6½" × 21", including seam allowances. Crosscut the strip set into four segments, 2½" × 6½".

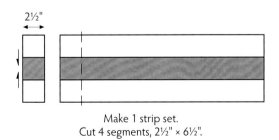

Make 1 strip set.
Cut 4 segments, 2½" × 6½".

3 Sew two segments from step 1 and one segment from step 2 together as shown to make a nine-patch unit. Repeat to make four matching units that measure 6½" square, including seam allowances.

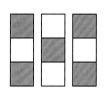

Make 4 units,
6½" × 6½".

4 Draw a diagonal line from corner to corner on the wrong side of each cream square. Place a marked square on one corner of a nine-patch unit, as shown. Sew on the marked lines. Trim the excess corner fabric, ¼" from the stitched line. In the same way, sew marked squares on the three remaining corners of the nine-patch unit to make a unit. Make four units that measure 6½" square, including seam allowances.

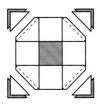

Make 4 units,
6½" × 6½".

5 From the remaining dark 2½" × 21" strip, cut one square, 1½" × 1½".

6 Lay out four units from step 4, four cream 1½" × 6½" rectangles, and the dark square from step 5 as shown. Sew the pieces together into rows. Join the rows to make a block. Repeat to make a total of 20 blocks that measure 13½" square, including seam allowances.

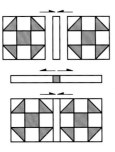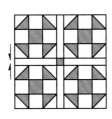

Make 20 blocks,
13½" × 13½".

assembling the quilt top

1 Join four blocks and three cream 1½" × 13½" rectangles as shown to make a block row. Make five rows that measure 13½" × 55½", including seam allowances.

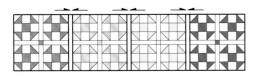

Make 5 rows,
13½" × 55½".

ROLLIN' WITH
Sherri McConnell

Rollin', rollin', rollin'... designer Sherri McConnell (AQuiltingLife.com) keeps it rollin' better than anyone we've seen! She's a steamroller when it comes to lining up her projects and getting 'em sewn.

When I'm sewing with a Jelly Roll, this is how I roll: Unroll the strips and separate them by color.

My favorite roll is a lobster roll!

In my dreams, the car I roll up the driveway in is a BMW 4 Series.

When I'm on a roll in my sewing room, I ignore my phone and just keep sewing!

Don't roll your eyes, but I often forget to change my sewing-machine needle.

If I'm rolling up my sleeves and getting ready for some serious sewing time, I make sure to eat and have snacks ready.

If I could roll back the clock, here's the advice I'd give my younger self: Don't waste time with worry.

Roll call for my "Sewing Must-Haves" would include these three things: A new rotary-cutter blade for my Olfa cutter, a clean cutting and pressing area, and a fantastic steam iron!

2 Join four cream 1½" × 13½" rectangles and three pink 1½" squares as shown to make a sashing row. Make four rows that measure 1½" × 55½", including seam allowances.

Make 4 rows,
1½" × 55½".

3 Lay out the block rows and sashing rows as shown in the quilt assembly diagram below. Join the rows to make the quilt-top center, which should measure 55½" × 69½", including seam allowances.

4 Join the cream 2"-wide strips end to end. From the pieced strip, cut two 69½"-long strips and two 58½"-long strips. Sew the 69½"-long strips to opposite sides of the quilt-top center. Sew the 58½"-long strips to the top and bottom of the quilt top. The quilt top should measure 58½" × 72½", including seam allowances.

5 Join the blue 3½"-wide strips end to end. From the pieced strip, cut two 72½"-long strips and two 64½"-long strips. Sew the 72½"-long strips to opposite sides of the quilt-top center. Sew the 64½"-long strips to the top and bottom of the quilt top. The quilt top should measure 64½" × 78½".

finishing the quilt

For more details about any finishing steps, visit ShopMartingale.com/HowtoQuilt.

1 Layer the quilt top, batting, and backing. Hand or machine quilt. Parfait is quilted with an allover pattern of circles within circles and includes petals that form a flower design in the smaller circles.

2 Use the pink 2¼"-wide strips to make the binding; attach it to the quilt.

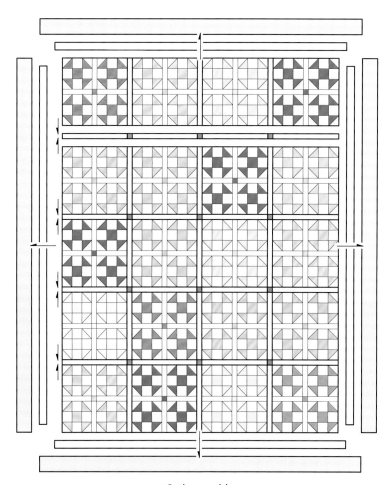

Quilt assembly

apricot jelly

BY COREY YODER

Do you love to savor each season's best bounty? Pick your favorite mix of strips and showcase them in a putty-colored fabric frame that makes your prints the starring attraction. It's like a glimpse of spring that brings a twinkle to your eye.

FINISHED QUILT: 68½" × 84½"
FINISHED BLOCK: 12" × 12"

materials

Yardage is based on 42"-wide fabric. Jelly Rolls contain 40 strips, 2½" × width of fabric.

1 Jelly Roll of assorted dark print strips for blocks and binding*

2¾ yards of white solid for blocks and sashing

2 yards of gray solid for sashing

5¼ yards of fabric for backing

77" × 93" piece of batting

If you want to use one fabric for the binding, you'll need ⅝ yard.

cutting

From the white solid, cut:

10 strips, 2½" × 42"; crosscut into 150 squares, 2½" × 2½"

43 strips, 1½" × 42"; crosscut into:
    98 strips, 1½" × 12½"
    240 squares, 1½" × 1½"

From *each* of the assorted dark print strips, cut:

1 rectangle, 2½" × 10½" (40 total)
1 rectangle, 2½" × 8½" (40 total)
1 rectangle, 2½" × 6½" (40 total)
1 rectangle, 2½" × 4½" (40 total)
1 square, 2½" × 2½" (40 total)

Set aside the leftover strips to use for the scrappy binding. The leftover strips need to be at least 9½" long after removing the selvages.

From the gray solid, cut:

5 strips, 1½" × 42"; crosscut into 120 squares, 1½" × 1½"
22 strips, 2½" × 42"; crosscut into:
    49 strips, 2½" × 12½"
    120 rectangles, 1½" × 2½"

making the blocks

Press all seam allowances in the direction indicated by the arrows.

1 Sew a white 2½" square to one end of a dark 2½" × 10½" rectangle to make a unit. Make 40 units that measure 2½" × 12½", including seam allowances.

Make 40 units,
2½" × 12½".

2 Join a dark square, a white 2½" square, and a dark 2½" × 8½" rectangle to make a unit. Make 40 units that measure 2½" × 12½", including seam allowances.

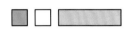 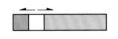

Make 40 units,
2½" × 12½".

3 Join a dark 2½" × 4½" rectangle, a white 2½" square, and a dark 2½" × 6½" rectangle to make a unit. Make 40 units that measure 2½" × 12½", including seam allowances.

Make 40 units,
2½" × 12½".

4 Lay out two units *each* from steps 1, 2, and 3, rotating the units as shown. Join the units to make a block. Make 20 blocks that measure 12½" square, including seam allowances.

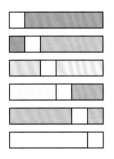 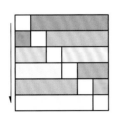

Make 20 blocks,
12½" × 12½".

making the sashing units

1 Draw a diagonal line from corner to corner on the wrong side of each white 1½" square. Place a marked square on one end of a gray 1½" × 2½" rectangle, right sides together. Sew on the marked line. Trim the excess corner fabric, ¼" from the stitched line. Place a marked square on the opposite end of the gray rectangle. Sew and trim as before to make a flying-geese unit. Make 120 units that measure 1½" × 2½", including seam allowances.

Make 120 units,
1½" × 2½".

2 Lay out four gray 1½" squares, four flying-geese units, and one white 2½" square in three rows as shown. Sew the squares and units together into rows. Join the rows to make a star unit. Make 30 units that measure 4½" square, including seam allowances.

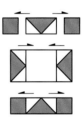

Make 30 units,
4½" × 4½".

3 Sew one gray 2½" × 12½" strip between two white 1½" × 12½" strips to make a sashing unit. Make 49 units that measure 4½" × 12½", including the seam allowances.

Make 49 units,
4½" × 12½".

Designed and pieced
by Corey Yoder.

Quilted by Kaylene Parry.

assembling the quilt top

1 Join five star units and four sashing units to make a sashing row. Make six rows that measure 4½" × 68½", including seam allowances.

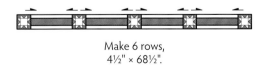

Make 6 rows,
4½" × 68½".

2 Join five sashing units and four blocks to make a block row. Make five rows that measure 12½" × 68½", including seam allowances.

Make 5 rows,
12½" × 68½".

3 Join the sashing rows and block rows, alternating them as shown in the quilt assembly diagram below. Stitch around the perimeter of the quilt top, ⅛" from the outer edges, to lock the seams in place.

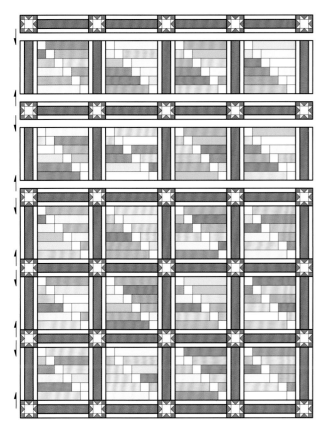

Quilt assembly

finishing the quilt

For more details about any finishing steps, visit ShopMartingale.com/HowtoQuilt.

1 Layer the quilt top, batting, and backing. Hand or machine quilt. Apricot Jelly is quilted with an allover design of curved lines.

2 Trim the leftover dark strips to measure 2¼" × 9½". Join the strips end to end to make the binding; attach it to the quilt.

ROLLIN' WITH
Corey Yoder

Hey, hey! Corey Yoder (CorianderQuilts.com) is rolling in style with some savvy advice for sewing up a storm.

When I'm sewing with a Jelly Roll, this is how I roll: My quilts are either totally unplanned and scrappy, or pieced with a little bit of a plan.

My favorite roll is mmm . . . a cinnamon roll all the way!

In my dreams, the car I roll up the driveway in is a Jeep Wrangler.

When I'm on a roll in my sewing room, I listen to podcasts.

Don't roll your eyes, but I'm in bed by 9 p.m. Early to bed, early to rise.

If I'm rolling up my sleeves and getting ready for some serious sewing time, I make sure to cut out all of my pattern pieces ahead of time.

If I could roll back the clock, here's the advice I'd give my younger self: Don't take yourself so seriously.

Roll call for my "Sewing Must-Haves" would include these three things: Clearly Perfect Angles static sewing guide, comfy sewing clothes, and a Clover thread-cutter pendant.

rule the roost

BY ANNE SUTTON

We knew we wouldn't have to egg you on to create your very own henhouse filled with strippy chicks. Each hen has a story to tell with colorful prints. The quilt is so cute, we're all clucking over it!

FINISHED QUILT: 40½" × 40½"
FINISHED CHICKEN BLOCK: 8" × 8"
FINISHED NINE PATCH BLOCK: 3" × 3"

materials

Yardage is based on 42"-wide fabric. Jelly Rolls contain 40 strips, 2½" × width of fabric.

1 Jelly Roll of assorted prints for appliqués and sashing squares

⅞ yard of cream solid for blocks

½ yard of brown dot for sashing

¼ yard of red dot for inner border and Nine Patch blocks

½ yard of cream dot for outer border

½ yard of red check for binding

2⅝ yards of fabric for backing

47" × 47" piece of batting

Water-soluble marker or fabric pencil

Brown embroidery floss

cutting

Choose 9 sets of 4 assorted print strips (36 total), making sure you like the way the strips blend together. Each set of strips will be used to make 1 chicken body.

From *each* of the 36 assorted print strips for chickens, cut:
1 strip, 2½" × 12" (36 total)

From the remaining assorted print strips, cut a *total* of:
16 squares, 2½" × 2½"

From the cream solid, cut:
3 strips, 8½" × 42"; crosscut into 9 squares, 8½" × 8½"
16 squares, 1½" × 1½"

From the brown dot, cut:
6 strips, 2½" × 42"; crosscut into 24 strips, 2½" × 8½"

From the red dot, cut:
5 strips, 1½" × 42"; crosscut into:
    2 strips, 1½" × 34½"
    2 strips, 1½" × 32½"
    20 squares, 1½" × 1½"

From the cream dot, cut:
4 strips, 3½" × 42"; crosscut into 4 strips, 3½" × 34½"

From the red check, cut:
5 strips, 2¼" × 42"

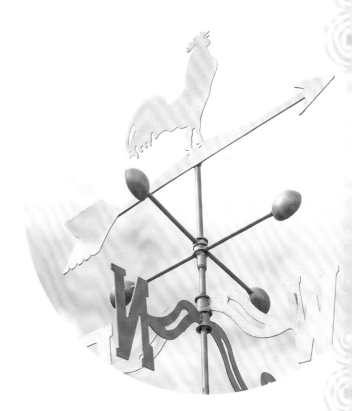

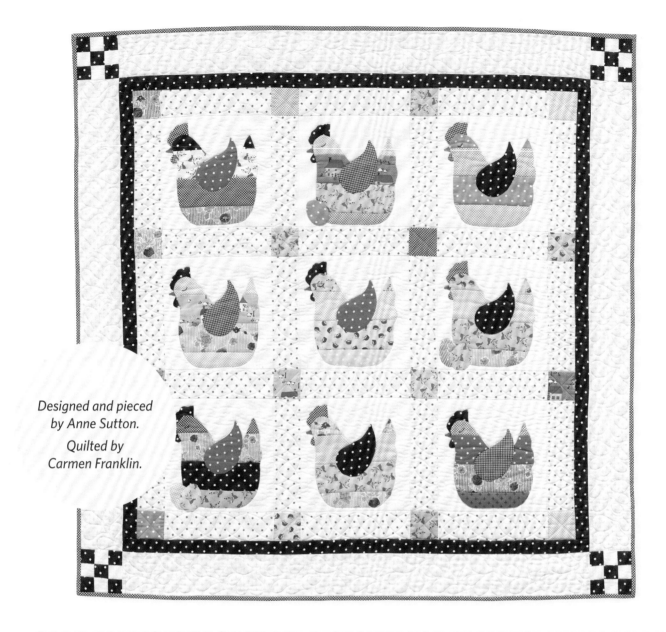

Designed and pieced by Anne Sutton.

Quilted by Carmen Franklin.

appliquéing the blocks

The appliqué patterns are on page 65. Use your favorite appliqué method. The instructions are written for turned-edge appliqué. Use a very narrow blind-hem stitch and matching thread to secure the pieces. Or, you can hand appliqué the pieces to secure them. Reverse the patterns for fusible appliqué. Press all seam allowances in the direction indicated by the arrows.

1 Sew one set of four print 2½" × 12" strips together along their long edges to make a strip unit. Make nine units that measure 8½" × 12", including seam allowances.

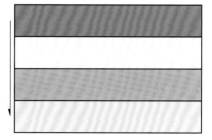

Make 9 units, 8½" × 12".

2 Use the chicken pattern and the strip units to prepare nine chicken bodies, adding a scant ¼" seam allowance all around the perimeter.

3 Select two different print strips for the combs and waddles, one print strip for the beaks, and three different print strips for the wings. Use the patterns to prepare nine combs and waddles, nine beaks, and nine wings, adding a scant ¼" seam allowance all around the perimeter. Using assorted print strips, prepare five eggs for appliqué.

4 Place the chicken pattern and one chicken body on a light box or bright window. Use a water-soluble marker or fabric pencil to trace the eye onto the chicken.

5 Center a chicken body on a cream 8½" square, placing the bottom of the chicken ½" up from the bottom edge of the block. Add the comb, beak, and waddle, and appliqué them in place. Appliqué the chicken body and then the wing. Make nine blocks that measure 8½" square, including seam allowances. Referring to the photo on page 62, appliqué the eggs to three of the blocks.

6 Use brown embroidery floss and a backstitch to embroider the eye on each chicken.

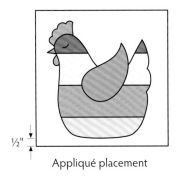

½"

Appliqué placement

assembling the quilt top

1 Join three blocks and four brown strips as shown to make a block row. Make three rows that measure 8½" × 32½", including seam allowances.

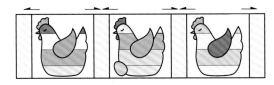

Make 3 rows,
8½" × 32½".

2 Join four print 2½" squares and three brown strips as shown to make a sashing row. Make four rows that measure 2½" × 32½", including seam allowances.

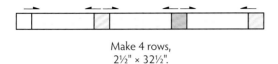

Make 4 rows,
2½" × 32½".

3 Lay out the block rows and sashing rows as shown in the quilt assembly diagram at right. Join the rows to make the quilt-top center, which should measure 32½" square, including seam allowances.

4 Sew red 1½" × 32½" strips to opposite sides of the quilt-top center. Sew red 1½" × 34½" strips to the top and bottom of the quilt top, which should measure 34½" square, including seam allowances.

5 Join five red squares and four cream 1½" squares to make a Nine Patch block. Make four blocks that measure 3½" square, including seam allowances.

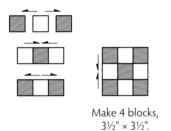

Make 4 blocks,
3½" × 3½".

6 Sew cream dot 3½" × 34½" strips to opposite sides of the quilt. Sew a Nine Patch block to the ends of each remaining cream dot strip. Sew these to the top and bottom of the quilt top, which should measure 40½" square.

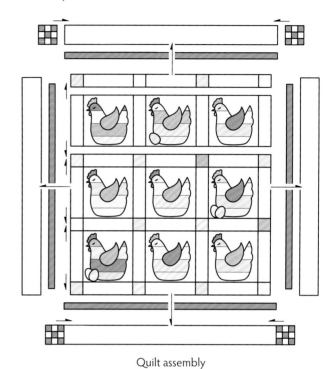

Quilt assembly

finishing the quilt

For more details about any finishing steps, visit ShopMartingale.com/HowtoQuilt.

1 Layer the quilt top, batting, and backing. Hand or machine quilt. Rule the Roost is quilted in the ditch around the chickens and with straight lines in the background. Curved lines are quilted in the sashing and a floral motif in the outer border.

2 Use the red check 2¼"-wide strips to make the binding; attach it to the quilt.

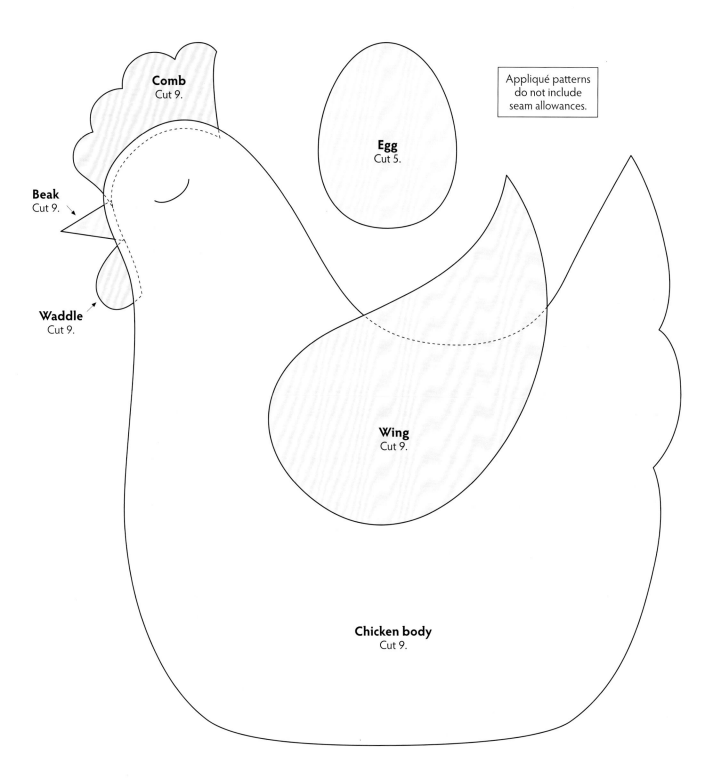

Comb
Cut 9.

Egg
Cut 5.

Appliqué patterns
do not include
seam allowances.

Beak
Cut 9.

Waddle
Cut 9.

Wing
Cut 9.

Chicken body
Cut 9.

mountain climbing

BY BETSY CHUTCHIAN

You'll have fun sorting your scrappy strips into mountains of colorful piles. Choose two contrasting colors that complement one another, then set one color pointing north and the other pointing south to create a field of colorful peaks.

FINISHED SIZE: 54½" × 64½"
FINISHED BLOCK: 9" wide (at base) × 8" tall

materials

Yardage is based on 42"-wide fabric. Jelly Rolls contain 40 strips, 2½" × width of fabric.

1 Jelly Roll of assorted prints for blocks

2⅜ yards of gray print for setting triangles

½ yard of black print for binding

3½ yards of fabric for backing

61" × 71" piece of batting

Template plastic

Mini 60° Triangle by EZ Quilting (optional)

Hex N More ruler by Jaybird Quilts (optional)

cutting

From the gray print, cut:
9 strips, 8½" × 42"

From the black print, cut:
7 strips, 2¼" × 42"

preparing the triangles

If you are using a Mini 60° Triangle and a Hex N More ruler, you don't need to make the A and B templates in step 1.

1 Trace each of the A, B, and C triangle patterns on pages 70 and 71 onto template plastic. Cut out the templates on the marked line to make one of each template.

2 Fold each print strip in half crosswise. Use template A to cut 20 A triangles from each strip (800 total; 768 are needed so 32 will be extra), rotating the template as shown. Be sure to trim the corners as indicated on the template.

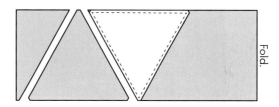

Cut 800 A triangles.

3 In the same way, use template B to cut 40 B triangles from seven of the gray 8½"-wide strips.

4 Use template C to cut eight C triangles and eight reversed C triangles from the remaining gray strips as shown.

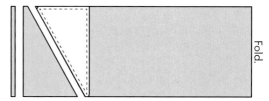

Cut 8 and 8 reversed C triangles.

*Designed and pieced
by Betsy Chutchian.*

Quilted by Karen Wood.

assembling the quilt top

Select 10 dark A triangles and six light or medium
A triangles for each block. You may want to reverse the
light and dark triangles in some blocks. Press all seam
allowances in the direction indicated by the arrows.

1 Lay out 16 A triangles in four rows as shown.
Sew the triangles together into rows. Join the
rows to make a block. Make 48 blocks.

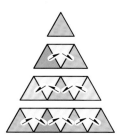
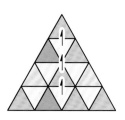

Make 48.

2 Lay out the blocks, B triangles, C triangles, and C reversed triangles in eight rows as shown in the quilt assembly diagram below. Sew the blocks and triangles together into rows. Join the rows to make the quilt top, which should measure 54½" × 64½", including seam allowances. Stitch around the perimeter of the quilt top, ⅛" from the outer edges, to lock the seams in place.

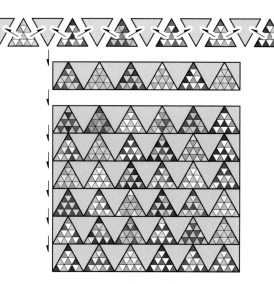

Quilt assembly

finishing the quilt

For more details about any finishing steps, visit ShopMartingale.com/HowtoQuilt.

1 Layer the quilt top, batting, and backing. Hand or machine quilt. Mountain Climbing is quilted with an allover pattern of wavy lines that form switchbacks across the quilt.

2 Use the black 2¼"-wide strips to make the binding; attach it to the quilt.

ROLLIN' WITH
Betsy Chutchian

If you love to roll back the clock and appreciate the timeless appeal of reproduction quilts and the familiar patterns of days gone by, then you might well be a kindred spirit of designer Betsy Chutchian (BetsysBestQuiltsandMore.blogspot.com).

When I'm sewing with a Jelly Roll, this is how I roll: First, I use a lint roller or packing tape to remove the fuzzy fluff from the edges. Then I unroll and spray the folded strips with Best Press or a non-aerosol spray starch, and press each one before cutting.

My favorite roll is a cinnamon roll.

In my dreams, the car I roll up the driveway in is my 1969 yellow Ford Mustang that I foolishly sold.

When I'm on a roll in my sewing room, I don't get up to snack.

Don't roll your eyes, but I only change sewing-machine needles when they break, rarely oil whatever is supposed to be oiled on a sewing machine, and stitch over pins.

If I'm rolling up my sleeves and getting ready for some serious sewing time, I make sure to have my husband order pizza or pick up burgers.

If I could roll back the clock, here's the advice I'd give my younger self: Take more time to enjoy the moment, and don't spend it looking back and saying, "I wish I had . . . ."

Roll call for my "Sewing Must-Haves" would include these three things: Olfa Frosted Advantage rulers, a hot iron with steam, and Netflix on my Kindle.

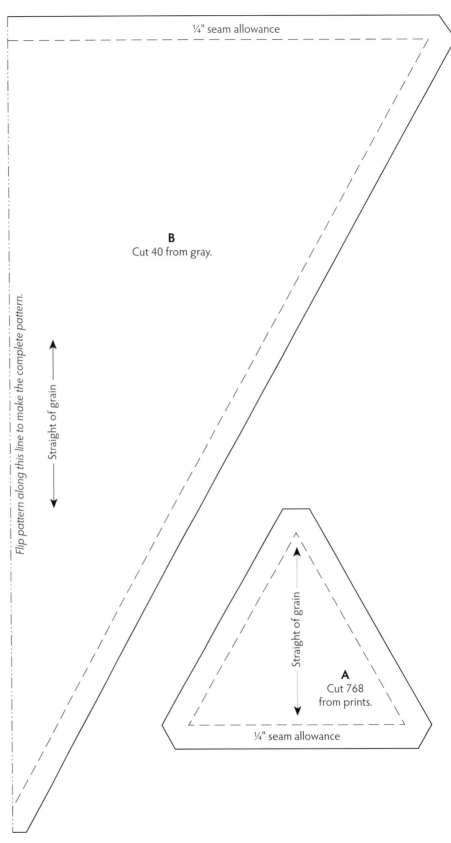

¼" seam allowance

Flip pattern along this line to make the complete pattern.

Straight of grain

B
Cut 40 from gray.

Straight of grain

A
Cut 768
from prints.

¼" seam allowance

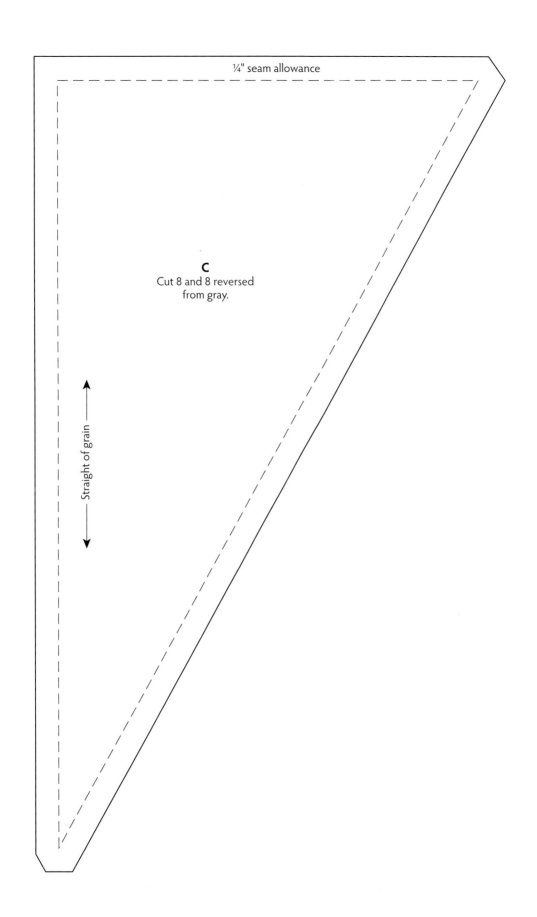

¼" seam allowance

C
Cut 8 and 8 reversed
from gray.

Straight of grain

maisy daisies

BY JOANNA FIGUEROA

Maisy, Maisy, it's not crazy. How does your garden grow? With little strips and lots of trips to the fabric store to-and-fro. Okay, maybe it's not quite like that, but who doesn't love a trip to the quilt shop to choose fabrics? Cultivate them into your own patchwork posies and dig in!

FINISHED QUILT: 56⅛" × 71½"
FINISHED BLOCK: 9" × 9"

materials

Yardage is based on 42"-wide fabric. Jelly Rolls contain 40 strips, 2½" × width of fabric.

6 Jelly Roll strips of assorted red prints for Flower blocks and leaf units

7 Jelly Roll strips of assorted green prints for Flower blocks and leaf units

4 Jelly Roll strips of assorted yellow prints for Flower blocks and leaf units

3 Jelly Roll strips of assorted cream prints A for Flower blocks and leaf units

4 Jelly Roll strips of assorted gray prints for Flower blocks and leaf units

16 Jelly Roll strips of assorted cream prints B for sashing columns

1½ yards of ivory solid for background

¼ yard of green solid for stems

⅞ yard of yellow solid for border

½ yard of green diagonal stripe for binding

3½ yards of fabric for backing

63" × 78" piece of batting

cutting

From *each* of 3 red print strips, cut:
1 strip, 2½" × 34" (3 total)
3 squares, 2" × 2" (9 total)

From *each* of the 3 remaining red print strips, cut:
4 rectangles, 2" × 3½" (12 total)
13 squares, 2" × 2" (39 total)

From *each* of 6 green print strips, cut:
1 strip, 2½" × 34" (6 total)
1 rectangle, 2" × 3½" (6 total)
1 square, 2" × 2" (6 total)

From the 1 remaining green print strip, cut:
2 rectangles, 2" × 3½"
2 squares, 2" × 2"

From *each* of the yellow print strips, cut:
1 strip, 2½" × 34" (4 total)
3 squares, 2" × 2" (12 total)

From *each* of the cream print A strips, cut:
1 strip, 2½" × 34" (3 total)

From *each* of the gray print strips, cut:
1 strip, 2½" × 34" (4 total)
1 rectangle, 2" × 3½" (4 total)
1 square, 2" × 2" (4 total)

Continued on page 74

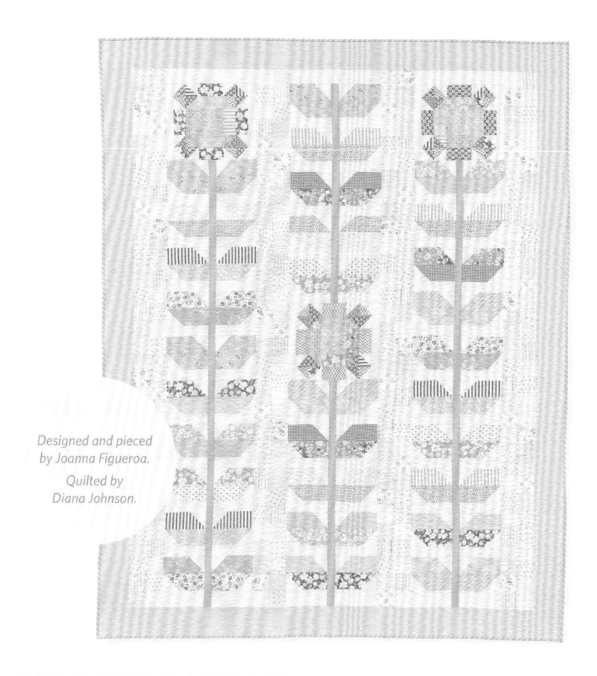

*Designed and pieced
by Joanna Figueroa.*

*Quilted by
Diana Johnson.*

Continued from page 73

From the ivory solid, cut:

8 strips, 1¾" × 42"; crosscut into 54 rectangles, 1¾" × 5½"
9 strips, 2½" × 42"; crosscut into:
    6 rectangles, 2½" × 5½"
    120 squares, 2½" × 2½"
1 strip, 2¼" × 42"; crosscut into 3 rectangles, 2¼" × 11⅜"
2 strips, 2" × 42"; crosscut into 36 squares, 2" × 2"
2 strips, 1½" × 42"; crosscut into 6 rectangles, 1½" × 9½"

From the green solid, cut:

5 strips, 1⅜" × 42"; crosscut *2 strips* into:
    1 strip, 1⅜" × 27½"
    1 strip, 1⅜" × 26¾"

From the yellow solid, cut:

7 strips, 4" × 42"

From the green stripe, cut:

7 strips, 2¼" × 42"

making the leaf units

Press all seam allowances in the direction indicated by the arrows.

1 Sew the red, green, yellow, cream, and gray 2½" × 34" strips together in pairs to make 10 strip sets that measure 4½" × 34", including seam allowances. Crosscut each strip set into six 4½" × 5½" segments (60 total).

Make 10 strip sets.
Cut 6 segments, 4½" × 5½" (60 total).

2 Draw a diagonal line from corner to corner on the wrong side of the ivory 2½" squares. Place marked squares on opposite corners of a segment from step 1 as shown. Sew on the marked lines. Trim the excess corner fabric ¼" from the stitched line. Repeat to sew marked squares on opposite corners of a matching segment from step 1 as shown. Trim and press. Make 30 of each leaf unit. The units should measure 4½" × 5½", including seam allowances.

Make 30 of each,
4½" × 5½".

making the flower blocks

You'll make three Flower blocks, two with green inner circles and one with a gray inner circle.

1 Join four yellow 2" squares to make a four-patch unit. Make three units that measure 3½" square, including seam allowances.

Make 3 units,
3½" × 3½".

2 Join four red 2" squares to make a four-patch unit. Make 12 units that measure 3½" square, including seam allowances.

Make 12 units,
3½" × 3½".

3 Draw a diagonal line from corner to corner on the wrong side of each green print, gray print, and ivory solid 2" square. Place marked ivory and green (or gray) squares on opposite corners of a red four-patch unit as shown. Sew on the marked lines. Trim the excess corner fabric, ¼" from the stitched line. Repeat to sew marked ivory squares on the remaining two corners of the unit. Make 12 units that measure 3½" square, including seam allowances.

Make 12 units,
3½" × 3½".

4 Join red and green (or red and gray) 2" × 3½" rectangles to make a unit. Make 12 units that measure 3½" square, including seam allowances.

Make 12 units,
3½" × 3½".

press strip sets

When pressing strip sets, carefully watch for two things. One, take care to press the strips completely open so you don't lose fabric in the seams. Two, make sure the strip set is completely straight, without waves or curving. This will ensure accurate pieces when you're done.

5 Lay out four units from step 3, four units from step 4 that have matching red rectangles, and one yellow four-patch unit in three rows as shown. Sew the units together into rows. Join the rows to make a block. Make one gray and two green blocks, which should measure 9½" square, including seam allowances.

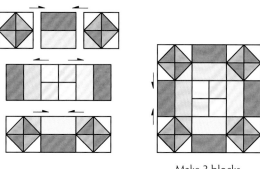

Make 3 blocks,
9½" × 9½".

6 Sew ivory 1½" × 9½" rectangles to opposite sides of each block. Trim the blocks to measure 9½" × 11⅜", including seam allowances.

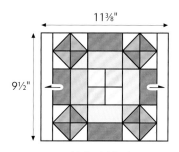

Make 3 blocks.

making the stem units

1 Join three green 1⅜" × 42" strips end to end. From the pieced strip, cut two 53¾"-long strips.

2 Lay out 10 sets of leaf units, 18 ivory 1¾" × 5½" rectangles, and one green 53¾"-long strip as shown, making sure to place matching leaf units on opposite sides of the green strip. Sew the leaf units and ivory rectangles together to make two columns. Sew an ivory 2½" × 5½" rectangle to the bottom of each column. The columns should measure 5½" × 53¾", including seam allowances. Sew the green strip between the leaf columns to make the left stem unit, which should measure 11⅜" × 53¾", including seam allowances. Repeat to make the right stem unit.

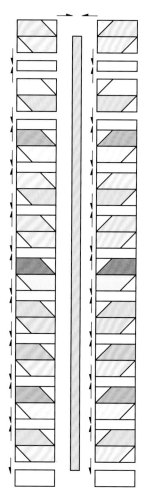

Make 2 units,
11⅜" × 53¾".

3 Lay out five sets of leaf units, 10 ivory 1¾" × 5½" rectangles, and the green 26¾"-long strip, matching the leaf units as before. Sew the leaf units and ivory rectangles together. Sew the green strip between the leaf columns to make the top-center stem unit, which should measure 11⅜" × 26¾", including seam allowances.

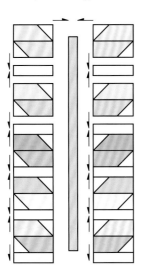

Top-center stem unit.
Make 1 unit, 11⅜" × 26¾".

4 Lay out five sets of leaf units, eight ivory 1¾" × 5½" rectangles, and the green 27½"-long strip, matching the leaf units as before. Sew the leaf units and ivory rectangles together. Sew an ivory 2½" × 5½" rectangle to the bottom of each column. Sew the green strip between the leaf columns to make the bottom-center stem unit, which should measure 11⅜" × 27½", including seam allowances.

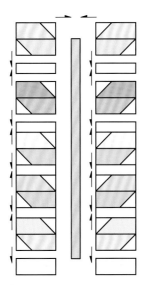

Bottom-center stem unit.
Make 1 unit, 11⅜" × 27½".

ROLLIN' WITH
Joanna Figueroa

She's rolling in clover . . . er, maybe daisies! Either way, Joanna Figueroa (FigTreeandCompany.com) has so many bloomin' ideas for adorable quilts she's cultivating, that we're just happy we're able to pluck this one from her creative mind!

When I'm sewing with a Jelly Roll, this is how I roll: I usually don't unroll them, just pet them. But if I have to unroll, I pair them almost immediately as I usually start with pairs for one design or another.

My favorite roll is a seeded sourdough roll. Pretty much any roll with lots of seeds on it and I'm good. I'm not a huge fan of sweet rolls . . . I'm weird that way.

In my dreams, the car I roll up the driveway in is a vintage convertible Mustang. One day . . . .

When I'm on a roll in my sewing room, I am totally in the zone and perhaps on another planet. I don't hear phone calls, remember appointments, or remember to feed the family. It's a good thing my husband is a hands-on kind of dad and can make dinner as well as I can!

If I'm rolling up my sleeves and getting ready for some serious sewing time, I make sure I find something good on Netflix (and it has to have more than just a couple seasons so I can really get into it). I also make sure I have loads of iced tea either already made or ready to make, and usually that my house is quiet and empty of other people . . . or at least that they don't need me for anything.

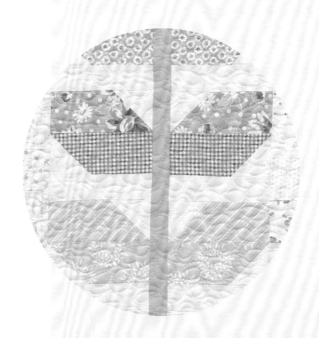

making the sashing columns

① Sew four cream B 2½" × 42" strips together along their long edges to make a strip set that measures 8½" × 42". Make four strip sets and crosscut each strip set into 16 segments (64 total), 2½" × 8½", including seam allowances.

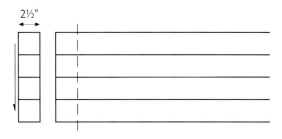

Make 4 strip sets.
Cut 64 segments, 2½" × 8½".

② Join eight segments from step 1 end to end to make a strip. Make eight strips that measure 2½" × 64½", including seam allowances.

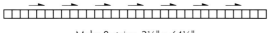

Make 8 strips, 2½" × 64½".

③ Join two strips from step 2 to make a sashing column. Make four columns that measure 4½" × 64½", including seam allowances.

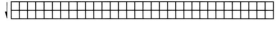

Make 4 columns, 4½" × 64½".

assembling the quilt top

① Lay out the blocks and stem units as shown in the quilt assembly diagram above right. Join the blocks and stem units to make a flower column. Make three columns. Then sew an ivory 2¼" × 11⅜" rectangle to the top of each column. The columns should measure 11⅜" × 64½", including seam allowances.

② Join the flower columns and sashing columns to make the quilt-top center, which should measure 49⅛" × 64½", including seam allowances.

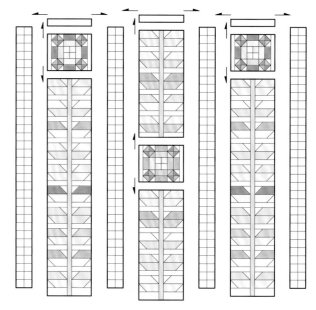

Quilt assembly

③ Join the yellow 4"-wide strips end to end. From the pieced strip, cut two 64½"-long strips and two 56⅛"-long strips. Sew the 64½"-long strips to opposite sides of the quilt-top center. Sew the 56⅛"-long strips to the top and bottom of the quilt top. The quilt top should measure 56⅛" × 71½".

finishing the quilt

For more details about any finishing steps, visit ShopMartingale.com/HowtoQuilt.

① Layer the quilt top, batting, and backing. Hand or machine quilt. Maisy Daisies is quilted with an allover feather design and crosshatching in the flower centers.

② Use the green striped 2¼"-wide strips to make the binding; attach it to the quilt.

meet the moda all-stars

LISA BONGEAN

A designer for Moda Fabrics, Lisa loves quilting, gardening, reading, and hunting for antiques. She and her husband, Nick, own Primitive Gatherings Quilt Shop and travel to quilting shows where Lisa teaches and shares her designs. You can find her at PrimitiveGatherings.us.

BETSY CHUTCHIAN

Betsy is an author, a designer for Moda Fabrics, and the cofounder of the 19th-Century Patchwork Divas. She developed a passionate interest in fabric, quilts, sewing, and history as a child. Betsy began teaching quiltmaking in 1990 and enjoys sharing her passion for reproducing 19th-century quilts. Visit her at BetsysBestQuiltsandMore.blogspot.com.

JANET CLARE

Inspired by children and their innocence and joy, Janet creates lively designs for quilts and embroidery. She is an author and a fabric designer who hosts workshops to share her creative techniques and design process. A mother of two, Janet lives in England and enjoys quilting, knitting, drawing, gardening, and other pastimes. Visit her at JanetClare.co.uk.

KARLA EISENACH

Karla and her daughters, Lisa Burnett and Susan Kendrick, are the creative minds behind Sweetwater, a design company in Colorado. Sweetwater started out as a scrapbook business and has now evolved to include fabric design, quilt patterns, kits, and more. Discover the latest at TheSweetwaterCo.com.

JOANNA FIGUEROA

For Joanna, quilting is the perfect combination of art and practicality. Joanna produces quilting and sewing patterns, block-of-the-month programs, and kits for her business, Fig Tree and Company. She has also designed over 40 fabric lines for Moda Fabrics. Find out more at FigTreeandCompany.com.

LYNNE HAGMEIER

A passion for vintage quilts inspired Lynne to take her first quilting class in 1987. Working in a quilt shop and stitching small quilts to sell led to selling patterns for the quilts she designed. Lynne has been designing popular fabric lines for Moda Fabrics since 2000. You can visit her at KTQuilts.com.

BRIGITTE HEITLAND

Brigitte is a textile and interior designer, the owner of Zen Chic, and a fabric designer for Moda Fabrics. She learned to sew while growing up in Germany and eventually started her own online quilting shop and long-arm business. Brigitte debuted her brand, Zen Chic, at the Spring Quilt Market 2011 trade show, where her eye-catching booth won an award. Visit BrigitteHeitland.de.

STACY IEST HSU

Stacy is a textile and product designer who has designed items for GapKids, Target, Tiny Prints, and others. She is now a designer for Moda Fabrics, and she also markets her own line of original designs. In her free time, Stacy enjoys spending time with her family, at the beach, and in her garden and yard. Visit StacyIestHsu.com.

SANDY KLOP

Sandy was trained as an art teacher and began quilting in 1979 while living in Iran and then Saudi Arabia, teaching at an American school. Back in California in 1984, she continued to build her interest in quilting. In 2002 she began creating her own designs, American Jane Patterns, and soon became a designer for Moda Fabrics. Visit AmericanJane.com.

SHERRI MCCONNELL

Sherri received her first sewing machine when she was about 10 years old and has been sewing clothing and home-decor items ever since. After receiving a "gentle push" from her grandmother, she branched out into quilting and hasn't stopped. You can find Sherri at AQuiltingLife.com.

LINZEE MCCRAY

Curiosity has led Linzee to explore a variety of vocational paths, including a career in journalism. After 13 years as a writer and editor, Linzee began freelancing, writing on topics such as textiles, crafts, and art. She loves gardening, hiking, reading, and of course, quilting. You can find Linzee on Instagram @seamswrite.

ME AND MY SISTER DESIGNS

Sisters Barbara Groves and Mary Jacobson make up the popular design team of Me and My Sister Designs. In addition to a line of quilt patterns, they have designed several fabric lines for Moda Fabrics. Their designs have been featured in *American Patchwork & Quilting* and *Quilter's Newsletter* magazine. Visit MeandMySisterDesigns.com.

ANNE SUTTON

Anne has always loved sewing and crafts, especially appliqué. For her, designing for Moda Fabrics is a dream come true. Anne's fabric style ranges from sweet sophistication to whimsical. She spends her days surrounded by pets in her Northern California loft studio. You can visit Anne at BunnyHillDesigns.com.

COREY YODER

A quilty mom of two girls and wife to one great husband, Corey enjoys playing with fabric in the form of quilts and quilt design. You can find her at CorianderQuilts.com.